FOOTBALL, FREEDOM AND PARADISE!

# RUDI VATA

My Story

FOOTBALL, FREEDOM AND PARADISE!

# RUDI VATA

## My Story

with Gerard McDade

Foreword by Paul McStay

pitch

First published by Pitch Publishing, 2024

Pitch Publishing
9 Donnington Park,
85 Birdham Road,
Chichester, West Sussex,
PO20 7AJ
www.pitchpublishing.co.uk
info@pitchpublishing.co.uk



A CIP catalogue record is available for this book from the British Library.

ISBN 978 1 80150 739 4

MIX
Paper | Supporting responsible forestry
FSC® C013604

Printed and bound in the UK on FSC® certified paper in line with our continuing commitment to ethical business practices, sustainability and the environment.

Typesetting and origination by Pitch Publishing

Printed and bound by CPI Anthony Rowe, UK

# CONTENTS

*'In a sense, when I look at my life, I sometimes feel as if I have lived* ***two*** *lives in one existence.'*

*Rudi Vata.*

*Shkoder, 2024*

# FOREWORD
## by Paul McStay

Rudi Vata stands as a symbol of perseverance and hope. His story is one of the most remarkable and intriguing football career pathways I've ever known. There was no recruitment process, just a burning desire to escape the oppressive dictatorial regime under which he learned to play football.

With a resolute spirit, Rudi made the courageous decision to transition from the theatre of international football at the Parc des Princes – where he faced the world's football luminaries like Michel Platini, Eric Cantona, and Didier Deschamps – to the unadorned reality of a refugee camp. It was the unbearable conditions in his beloved Albania that propelled him to make that decision, fuelled by determination to carve out a better life for himself.

This unwavering determination and the keen eye of Celtic manager Liam Brady guided Rudi to Celtic Park and a professional contract with Celtic Football Club. It was a privilege to work alongside Rudi during this important period in his career. Unfortunately, his time at Celtic coincided with some of the club's darkest days. Those were times that tested a player's inner strength, where continuing to perform on the pitch required immense resilience amidst the surrounding turmoil.

Throughout those challenging times, Rudi's resilience, professionalism, and sense of humour endeared him to his team-mates and Celtic supporters alike. It was great to have Rudi at the club not just from a football perspective but also from a fashion sense – his 70s dress style certainly took the pressure off me! Rudi soaked up the language, and his team-mates were more than happy to help him learn English, recommending shows like *Only an Excuse* and *Rab C Nesbitt*. Before long, he was one of the most fluent (sort of) English speakers in our first-team dressing room.

Rudi's resilience and determination played a crucial role in the 1995 Scottish Cup Final. In this critical match, Rudi contributed significantly to ending the club's years without a trophy. When Pierre van Hooijdonk headed home the cup-winning goal, it was a scene of emphatic jubilation. The football darkness and despair that had plagued the club and its fans lifted, but it was on Rudi's face that the real joy was most apparent. That smile came from a man who had truly seen darkness and desolation but had risen to hold the Scottish Cup as it glistened in the Hampden Park sunshine.

This victory was not just a triumph for the club but a personal testament to Rudi's incredible journey, resilience, and unwavering belief in a better future. Rudi's story reminds us that football is more than just a game – it is a lifeline and a pathway to achieving success against all odds. Rudi's journey from the oppressive conditions of Albania to the heights of Scottish football is an inspirational story, and an enduring testament to the power of perseverance.

**Paul McStay**
**– June 2024**

# PROLOGUE

In Albania, I lived close to the sea.

The Adriatic was our constant.

More than the gateway to trade, commerce, and potential freedom, it also served, to my father, as a metaphor for life.

Together, we would walk the shores and he would say to me:

*Life is like the sea. When the water is calm, there are beautiful moments, cool moments but then it can change.*

*Little waves can indicate those small problems in life and then the bigger waves can create a storm in the seas.*

*Difficult to ignore and laden with real dilemmas and problems. They may be difficult, but the key is to challenge those waves.*

*Remember – even a storm will tire, and you must ride it out until that moment.*

*Then, the days will be normal.*

And I listened.

CHAPTER 1

# REFUGEE

The Parc des Princes stadium in Paris on 30th March 1991 represented one of the highlights of my early football career.

Here was I, 21 years of age, taking to the pitch, representing my country against the cream of French international football at the time.

Among the ranks of 'Les Bleus' were names who would go on to make their mark on the European and global game.

The craft and leadership of Laurent Blanc, the fortress power of Basile Boli, the midfield intelligence of Luis Fernandez, the guile and finishing of Jean-Pierre Papin and then, the maverick talent that was Eric Cantona en route to making his genius felt in English football as well as on the continent.

All of them, under the command of their manager – unmistakably, one of the greatest French footballers of all time – Michel Platini.

These and men like them were the challenge that we, as proud Albanians, were having to face in order to compete on the international stage.

And yet – my own emotions were also in play, in the cauldron of the French national stadium.

I was a professional football player, concentrating on the game, but there were other issues.

Aleks had left abruptly.

Two years my elder, my brother had made the decision that it was time for him to leave Albania.

No one in my country, a beautiful country but one of repressive post-war communist dogma and brutal, torturous technique, took the decision to leave family, loved ones and friends lightly despite that repression.

It wasn't just a decision for oneself. You were making a decision with potential implications for the ones left behind and the punishment that *they* could suffer.

I had been tempted, *of course* I had, but the pull of my family was strong and, yet …

My belief was that it wasn't your fault if you were born into a country under dictatorship, but it was if you chose to accept it.

It wasn't your fault if you were born into poverty, but it was if you chose to do nothing about it.

Aleks had taken that chance, but I needed to know that he was safe and well.

I had much on my mind, so much to contemplate and I did so the night before the game against the French.

We, as a squad, were in Geneva and when morning came, the plan was to have breakfast and make our way across the border into France.

That plan became a little more challenging when we were informed by the hotel authorities that three of our squad had changed their clothes, picked up their rucksacks and gone for a 'walk' in the middle of the night. It was clear that they were not set on returning and our manager, a great man by the name of Bejkush Birce, had to shrug his shoulders and plan for a European Championship qualifier against one of the best nations on the planet with the bare bones of a 15-man squad now depleted by three.

To bolster the set-up, he called up a trio of players from the under-21 squad who were also competing in France that day. Not what you would call an ideal solution.

My memories of that night were of a hard match against an inspired opposition.

Two down in the first ten minutes, four by half-time, we rallied in the second half only to ship a fifth courtesy of an unfortunate own goal from Hysen Zmijani.

My team-mate would later be destined to play a part in my own plans, which I had now solidified.

Did my emotions affect my own personal performance that night?

Very probably, as my concentration was mixed with insecurity, but I completed my mission with what I like to think was dignity and I left the field of play clutching the jersey of no less than Eric Cantona, who offered it to me as a swap.

I had done my duty and served my country.

Our squad made its way back to the Hotel Concorde Montparnasse courtesy of the coach laid on by the French Football Federation.

Once back at the hotel, I picked up a sheet or two of the complimentary stationery as well as an envelope and pen as I set about writing the most difficult letter of my life.

How does one tell one's parents that you are leaving the country of your birth and their heritage to start a completely new life?

Through the letter I was able to impart to them that a group of Albanian immigrants from Belgium had informed me that Aleks was alive, well and relocated in Bari, Italy.

My parents had no telephone, so the letter was to be my only way to give them this information.

*'Aleks is alive and safe,'* I wrote, in my native Albanian. *'Please understand that this is my only moment to begin my future. Football will be my life – my chance for a professional career. When possible, and I hope soon, please come visit me in France and forgive me.'*

I slipped the letter into the envelope before placing it into my pocket and then I went looking for one man – my manager, Bejkush Birce.

He had always been good to me and now I felt I had to respect our relationship, by telling him that I was leaving.

Being the man he was, a man who had grown up in the post-war austerity of communist Albania, I felt he would understand my decision.

As a man of the world, he would also have known that there would be Communist Party members travelling with our squad as government officials – the *Sigurimi*.

Their duty would have been to ensure that we all returned to our homeland as well as ensuring that the defection of three of our players would not indicate a system going out of control.

*'I cannot come back. I need freedom,'* I said and Bejkush gave me an emotional hug and wished me well along with the very best of luck.

The next task was to entrust my envelope to another of my team-mates and he was the unfortunate scorer of the final French goal, Hysen Zmijani.

He and I had perspective. We knew the game was the game, but this was more important.

This was freedom, choice, and life.

Hysen assured me that he would fulfil the task for me and, secure in that knowledge, I left the hotel and went down into the Metro with another squad member, Adrian Sukaj, for company.

As I sat on the train, I contemplated that I was now heading into an unknown world and all I had with me were the clothes I stood in, the contents of my bag containing the football boots that were the tools of my trade, the key to my future, as well as the 50 American dollars (contraband currency in Albania) that nestled in the pocket of my jeans.

Adrian and I had been assured of the procedure by other immigrants and our route took us straight to the nearest police station, *Gendarmerie*.

Once inside, and in the hope that my fluency in Italian would be understood by the French police, I attempted to inform them that we were Albanian refugees and that we sought political asylum in their country.

With those words, my life would change forever, but in that moment, around 1am on the morning of 31 March 1991, we were taken through the procedure of detailing passport numbers and identification before being informed that an interpreter would be summoned, and we would be able to state our case.

Within 24 hours, Adrian and I were taken to a refugee camp in Nantes.

The camp was a symbol of equality.

It did not matter that, two days before, I had been on the international football stage – that I had been on the same pitch as Fernandez, Papin and Cantona, whose shirt was still lying in my bag – that I had represented my country and my people in front of thousands in the Parc des Princes as well as millions watching on television.

My new life starts here – where all are equal.

Like them, I am a refugee.

## CHAPTER 2

# ONE YEAR LATER

I would lie in bed at night and listen to my heart.

The training had been extremely tough and, having been told by my manager that this was to get me up to speed for the fast pace of the game, I accepted the challenge.

And so, as soon as I had finished the regular training session with the first-team squad and had taken my lunch, I was to report back out on the pitch with a fitness coach, Rab Douglas by name, who was dedicated to putting me through 100m sprints and 200m runs.

After two weeks, I would find myself lying in the bed of my hotel room, alone and with my body quite literally shaking from the exertion of it all.

As I lay out, I could honestly ask myself if I was going to die and, in my mind, I believed that I was happy to do so for this was the challenge – this was the game – and this was Celtic Football Club.

* * *

My route to Glasgow and one of the biggest club names in world football had been the direct result of one game that I had played in on 26 May 1992.

It was an international match, in Dublin, against the Republic of Ireland.

I had been in exile in France for over a year at that point and watched on as the break-up of the Eastern Bloc and the communist regime offered slow, but forward-moving momentum for Albania.

It had been an approach from Bejkush Birce that had brought me back into the fold, for it was a certainty that the old regime would not have sanctioned a call-up for me – a man they would have regarded as a traitor to his country.

The man who had embraced me warmly, almost as a father, one year before and wished me the 'best of luck' as I set off on my first genuine steps to freedom, had called me and asked me to come back to international football – come back and represent my country again in a series of World Cup qualifiers.

It was a plea that I could not and would not ignore.

Therefore, it was an emotional moment for me to return to my manager and team-mates, including Hyden Zmijani, who had delivered on his promise, at great personal risk, of taking that private letter to my parents in March 1991.

Possibly, I took that emotion that I carried out on to the pitch with me as my performance saw me named as the 'Man of the Match' in a narrow 2-0 defeat.

On the park that day for Ireland were players of the quality of Roy Keane, Paul McGrath, John Aldridge and a man who was soon destined to be my future team-mate although neither of us could have guessed it at the time, Irish goalkeeper Packie Bonner.

It was a former international team-mate of Packie's who was in charge of Celtic, Liam Brady, and I assume he had watched the game for, once I had returned to France, I was told to call him in Glasgow.

Here now was a call that would change both my professional and personal life.

A telephone call that set me on a path that sees me still living in Scotland with my wife, Annfrances of Wishaw and our two boys, Ruan and Rocco. Liam had played at the highest level and was an intelligent, articulate individual who, having left Arsenal as a hero of north London in 1980, had spent seven years playing his football with Juventus and a succession of other Italian clubs.

Typical of the man, as a dedicated professional, he had taken the trouble to become fluent in the language of the country where he earned his living and thus, as this Irishman sat behind the desk in his office in Glasgow, Scotland and I, an Albanian living in exile in Le Mans, France, spoke on the telephone, our exchange was in Italian.

How did I come to speak Italian? That can wait for another chapter.

Liam was interested in signing me and he didn't have to sell Celtic Football Club to me. Any student of the game knew about the Scottish powerhouse and their rich history.

On a personal level, I remember them coming to Albania in September 1979 to play Partizani Tirana in the European Cup. There was a lot of speculation that the club's talismanic captain, Danny McGrain, would be required to shave off his trademark beard as facial hair was not allowed in my home country, but for some reason, probably political, that did not happen.

I was ten years of age, daft for my football, and the fact that one of the biggest clubs in the world was coming to Albania was big news.

We only had one television channel in the country. Naturally, it was state-owned, and they showed the match live.

In the Celtic squad that day were Packie and another Celtic man who was destined to be my manager in the future, Tommy Burns.

Partizani won the match 1-0 through a goal by Agim Murati who, in his day, was renowned in Albania as the 'King of the air' for his ability to score headed goals.

At one point, in the second leg of the tie, in Glasgow, Partizani had an improbable early lead, an away goal and were 2-0 up on aggregate but Celtic rallied and ran out 4-1 winners on the night.

To be asked if I was interested in coming to Celtic was really not a question.

Of course, I wanted to come to this club – it was a fantastic opportunity for me.

I had prided myself on being fit but Liam told me immediately that I would need to get up to pace very quickly with Scottish football which, he felt, was much faster than the level I was used to in France, but if he wanted me and felt I could do a job for him then I was more than willing to make that investment.

Listen, I always knew I wasn't the greatest player in the world, but I was determined that nobody would match me for commitment and work ethic.

Those first few weeks were incredibly tough, but naturally, the body adjusts and, although there were moments in those early days when I questioned whether I had made the right move, my love of the game was an overriding factor in my life.

I was convinced that I could be successful.

Besides, it wasn't just for myself that I was at Celtic. I had become the first Albanian footballer to play in the British professional game and I saw that as a chance to fly a flag for my country and its people.

A bit of light for a country that, for so many years, had been in the darkness.

CHAPTER 3

# HERITAGE

The history of modern Albania has its roots in the events of the Second World War.

The Italian army, under the direction of the dictator, Benito Mussolini, invaded my country in 1939 with ambitions to extend his dominion throughout the Balkans, but was met with resistance.

Over a four-year period the Italians struggled to maintain their grip on the country and, weakening as a force, they ceded control in 1943 to Nazi Germany and, naturally, Adolf Hitler and his evil henchmen.

There now followed a brutal regime of forced labour, repression and economic exploitation which was the established footprint of the Nazi suppression.

The Partisans, under their charismatic leader, Enver Hoxha, mobilised resistance to the German forces and incredibly, by the end of 1944, had liberated my country from the Nazi yoke.

At the same time, Montenegro, a country bordering Albania, also succeeded in driving the Axis armies away, but in that particular conflict, my maternal grandmother, Jelena, a beautiful young wife with a baby daughter, Jovanka, lost her first husband to the ravages of war.

Like many wartime widows, she knew the hardship of trying to raise a child in a difficult environment and, although she was surrounded by her own family, that hardship was real and consistent.

The beauties of Montenegro, however, offered short respite from the grimness of war and, one day, Jelena took time to go to the beach with a few friends.

The Adriatic would be glistening, the sun burning and the roar of the waves crashing on to the shore would also be mixed with the sound of carefree voices seeking out some small vestige of enjoyment.

Into this scene, a party of cyclists arrived from Albania having cycled the roughly 44 kilometres to get to the beach.

Among them was Shuk Ashta – an Albanian businessman who owned a hotel in his hometown of Shkoder.

Shuk was an articulate, handsome man of the variety that might have been considered to be a bit of a playboy.

He embraced various interests, was a keen all-round sportsman and a talented jazz musician who played his music back in Shkoder.

A well-travelled figure, he knew his way around the great Italian cities such as Rome and Venice, where he had ventured on business trips.

His eye immediately fell upon this beautiful young Yugoslavian girl, and he knew that he had found the love of his life.

He gleaned what information he could from the local boys, but they did not know much about Jelena, so he made his own move.

The courtship was quick.

Jelena explained that she was a war widow with a child, a situation that she may have felt ruled out Shuk's advances, but he was not a man to be put off the scent so easily.

He had formulated his plans, proposed marriage to Jelena and asked her to come to live in Albania.

At that time, recently widowed and trying to raise a child, the offer would have been a tempting one, but still, leaving all her family behind to start a new life in another country – it was never going to be an easy decision.

And yet, she took it on, married Shuk, lived in Shkoder, and bore another three children, Sonya, Maria and Tatiana.

The eldest girl, Sonya, would be my mother.

If the decision to leave for Albania and a new life was a difficult one, then the closing of the country's borders in the post-war period presented another, possibly greater, challenge.

Enver Hoxha had risen to the top of the Communist Party on the back of his Partisan heroics although there was gossip that he had set up a rival to be eliminated during the conflict.

His name was Qemal Stafa, and, at one point, *he* was the Number One guy in the Party.

An intelligent man, he was also the boyfriend at the time of the girl who would later go on to become Hoxha's wife.

That seemed to convince many of the conspiracy theories surrounding the death of Qemal Stafa.

In time, Stafa would have a national football stadium named after him, but this may just have been a sop as there seemed little doubt that he died at the hands of his supposed comrade, Enver Hoxha. Such are the machinations of politics and power.

Whatever happened, Enver Hoxha was now the *numero uno* in the Communist Party.

With the title of First Secretary of the Party of Labour of Albania (PLA) he was, effectively, ruler and dictator of the country.

He had considerable power and, over the course of the next 40 years, wielded it mercilessly.

The first thing he did was to have a direct bearing on my family as he sealed the borders of the country and outlawed foreign travel.

There was a short period of grace for anyone who wanted to leave the country.

My grandmother Jelena now had three options. One, stay in Albania, raise her children but never see her family in Montenegro again. Two, return to Montenegro but only with Jovanka, as her other three children were classed as Albanian and would be prevented from leaving the country. Or three, stay in Albania but send Jovanka back to Montenegro, but, clearly, there was little choice at all.

I can only imagine the tortures she endured trying to make any decision from those options and in such a limited time period. At the end of it all, Jelena came to the conclusion that her best option was to remain in Albania and raise her family all together.

It was a decision that was to have a material impact on my life.

* * *

My father Pjeter was a respected man in Shkoder. As an official at the nationalised Bank of Albania, he would have advised on loans for the people of the city.

In later years, he would turn his hand to designing and building houses for those same people.

When he first met my mother, Sonya, I suspect he may have felt she would have been put off by the age difference between them, given that he would be some 12 years older than her and there was also a due process of courtship.

Pjeter informed my grandmother, Jelena, that he wanted to get to know Sonya better as he thought she was the best-looking girl in the city.

Jelena may also have entertained doubts as regards the age difference, but given her own experiences of hardship and the struggle to raise a family, she may also have regarded Pjeter as a safe option.

He was a respected banker – a man of the world – and she could see that he was an individual of character, good manners and pedigree.

She agreed to the courtship, and, after a suitable period, they were married in 1966.

A year later, my older brother, Aleks, was born and, on 13 February 1969, I arrived to complete the family.

Albania had been a closed-border country for over two decades by this time with the dictatorship of Enver Hoxha still in full vigour and the many restrictions placed upon my people by the state authorities were harsh, in some instances cruel and designed to keep individuals in their place.

For example, very few people were allowed to run a car and so the automobile my father owned sat rusting away in our garden for over 40 years.

As children Aleks and I quite naturally would play in it, pretending to drive and race a car across wide open landscapes. Perhaps, in a subconscious way, we were dreaming, even then, of freedom.

Dad's brother, Luigi, drove a taxi but even that was mostly restricted to the wintertime when the weather could become perilous for any form of travel.

The infrastructure was deliberately catastrophic in order to discourage any notion of ambition among the populace.

Indeed, 'ambition' was a dangerous word as it implied self-destiny and a right to self-determination – qualities that could lead to insurrection and revolution.

Houses were entitled to meagre domestic essentials such as a fridge, a freezer, a cooker and, in extremely rare cases, a television set although you could wait years for one and the only channel was state television. This served up a diet of Communist Party propaganda and state news that was deemed suitable for broadcasting and *manna* to the people.

In truth, the electricity connection was so poor that the country's national grid could not power much more than the domestic essentials that I have already mentioned along with the streetlamps that were set apart by 500 yards on the roads and were frequently turned off.

In the winter, Albania was cold and dark.

In the summer, when the temperatures would soar, there was no respite from the heat with any form of air-conditioning.

And yet, for all that, I can only describe my childhood as a happy one despite the fact that we had nothing, absolutely *nothing*, that could be described as having any material value.

I was raised in a good environment with loving parents, a close family and, in Aleks, I had a brother who would double as a friend.

We had the wealth of nature itself on our doorstep and considered ourselves lucky to have access to the healthy world of plums, peaches, cherries, figs and more that grew on the trees of our neighbourhood.

It was considered a vital tool of the Party that families would grow their own fruit and vegetables, and this dogma was meted out to all Albanians.

To this day, my mother continues to nurture her home produce of lemons, oranges and kiwi fruit.

Aleks and I would spend many days and nights playing in the fields and gardens, helping ourselves, possibly illegally, to the fruits of the earth that Mother Nature would provide with careful cultivation.

Quite without realising it, we were eating healthily, and this instilled in us the importance of good dietary practices.

Albania was beautiful.

We were ingrained to believe that it was the most beautiful country in the *world!*

And, of course, with so many of us having never been out of our country, we believed it.

Our 'freedoms' were curtailed, but as a boy, I naturally accepted this without argument.

If it was good enough for my parents, then it was good enough for Rudi.

CHAPTER 4

# THE GAME

I will always remember the lights in Holland.

Street lights.

Warm, welcoming, bright, and orange.

They seemed to celebrate life, freedom, and peace.

Yes, *peaceful.*

That was how I felt as I walked down the streets of Amsterdam, taking in the sights, breathing in the freedom that they offered to me.

It was a wonderland, a *dream*land.

I was not used to that, not at all.

All this freedom. The chance to walk the streets, drink in the culture, absorb the peace, the *difference.*

I had been raised to believe that Albania was the most beautiful country in the world. It was all that I needed in my life but now, at 18 years of age, I was experiencing something different, and it was stimulating my thoughts.

Making me think. Making me question.

And all of this had been brought to me by one vital thing: football.

I was in Holland as a member of the Albanian under-18 squad, to play in an international tournament.

In short, representing my country, but that country had taken me to a place where I could suddenly question everything that had gone before in Albania.

Of course, the authorities *knew* that.

They were well-versed in the system of oppression.

They understood that a group of young, healthy Albanian boys, suddenly in the heady freedom of western Europe, could struggle with all that had gone before, perhaps see a better way of life – and they were right.

As a consequence, we were closely shepherded, our movements watched – our eyes taking in the opulence of the Netherlands, but our *guardians* keeping a watchful, if somewhat, controlling eye over our every move and utterance.

The state police, *Sigurimi,* were a constant presence.

A dictatorship can control many things.

It can control your life, work, upbringing – everything.

Yet they could not control your thoughts.

I have already said that it was not one's choice to be born into a dictatorship, but it was one's choice to live in it.

And my choice was changing with one trip to Holland, to play football.

***

Football seemed to have been in my life from the earliest moment.

At five years of age, I vividly recall the 1974 World Cup tournament, in particular the brilliance of Holland, led by the outstanding player of his generation, Johan Cruyff. Of course, we did not have a television set in the house, but a close neighbour did and so we would gather around it, thrilled to be watching the greatest football competition on the planet.

Nowadays, there is a perception that the greatest players in the world ply their trade in the UEFA Champions League, but back then, we felt we were watching them in the biggest tournament in the world.

Cruyff was the standout. Naturally, I didn't understand the tactics or the formations, set plays et cetera, but I loved the game.

And, even now, as an adult, that Holland team would always go on to define what I felt football should be like – freedom of expression.

The Netherlands – the spawn of talent like Johan Neeskens, Rene van de Kerkhof, Rob Rensenbrink, Wim Van Hanegem, Johnny Rep and the man who would become my first real football hero – Ruud Krol.

Why Krol?

He was elegant, tough and stylish. A natural icon with his good looks and seemingly brooding temperament, but of course, we also shared a name in common. He was Ruud – I was Rudi. The only difference was the swapping of two vowels.

I adored Ruud and, on the day of the 1974 World Cup Final when I hoped that he and his team-mates would overcome the hosts, West Germany, I and a seeming cast of hundreds trotted over to my neighbour's house to watch the big match. Television sets were in meagre supply, so we were incredibly grateful to see the game.

Being so small, I had the advantage of being able to crawl through the mass of humanity and place myself directly in front of the set.

And there I lay, enthralled by the spectacle, listening to the roar of the crowd, drinking in the atmosphere as my heroes lost in a narrow 2-1 defeat to the West Germans.

East? West? Mere points on a compass. I was far too young to understand the politics of that divided country although, in time, I would appreciate the suffering of the East Germans and identify with it from my own experiences of a communist dogma.

And there he was, the imperious Franz Beckenbauer, the majestic *Kaiser* of the international game, standing tall and displaying the World Cup to his countrymen.

In time, he would become only the second man, after Brazilian Mario Zagallo, to win the trophy as both a player and a manager and, I am fortunate to say, that I would meet him much further down the road in my own football career.

But, in that moment, I felt the despair for Holland and my hero, Ruud Krol.

Such was my admiration that, on the cheap plastic school bag that we were given by the state when we entered the education system, I had written his name on the inside flap as a mark of my respect.

I felt that I, Rudi Vata of Albania, could become Ruud Krol of the Netherlands.

It was a secret inscription, of course, as I could not risk the possibility of it being discovered by anyone.

Imagine my horror, therefore, when my dad came across it one night when he routinely looked at my schoolwork.

Do you want to understand the effects of communist oppression?

Do you need to take on board an example of the fear it could induce in people?

All you had to do was to see my dad that night when he saw the inscription with my hero's name displayed across the interior of my satchel.

This was a man who had lived under the brutal heel of state control and genuinely feared for both me and the family if anyone had seen Ruud's name inside the flap of my bag.

The fear was genuine – the possibilities endless.

*What are you doing?* he said to me.

*Do you not understand how dangerous it is for you to display a name like this, so publicly? If you are caught, if* **we** *are caught, then there will be trouble.*

I was a child, barely able to tie my shoelaces and yet, I was being made to understand *the way that it was* for me, my family and my people.

To dream of being Ruud Krol, with all of his outrageous Dutch freedoms, to come and go as he pleased, sport a beard if he chose to do so and grow his hair to any length, was a sin punishable by the god of state control.

I learned my lesson and did not repeat it.

***

As a child, I was naturally active.

Sport engaged both me and Aleks.

In time, he would choose volleyball as his enthusiasm, but for me, it was always football.

I loved the game and looked out for any opportunity to play.

Naturally, there was no such thing as Christmas in Albania.

Three years before I was born, Enver Hoxha and the PLA tore down all the churches after already declaring that there was no such thing as religion and being religious. They had, of course, been putting Roman Catholic priests in jail throughout the course of the first 20 years of communist authority.

The clergy went undercover, but the *Sigurimi*, had their methods and networks which specialised in rooting out their undesirables.

I had been born into a Catholic family, but we were instructed by the state that being Albanian was a religion in itself.

We were to live our lives in that way.

Any attempt at practising our Catholic faith carried the threat of complete banishment to one of the many thousand bunkers, or *gulags*, and a prison life of torture and deprivation.

Many priests had suffered this fate, some never to be seen again.

My grandmother repeatedly warned me about making any religious utterance about God and, above all, no outward signs of faith, like blessing oneself in public.

That simple, inconspicuous act could, if seen by the wrong person, become potentially fatal to a person and a family.

No God.

No structured church.

No freedom to *believe* in a God.

All of that was considered dangerous, unpatriotic and an act of anti-communism.

No Christ, hence, no Christmas.

Stockings, presents, goodwill to all men with turkey dinners and lashings of wine and general celebration were not an option.

New Year's Eve was deemed instead to be the big festival in the Albanian calendar.

The national system was set up so that anyone who worked in the factories would be given presents for their children on that day. Innocuous little things like water pistols, skipping ropes et cetera.

That was *our* Christmas.

A time when we could, perhaps, if we were lucky, hope for a present. There was never any doubt what I wanted in those early years … a ball.

A football.

Nothing elaborate, of course. Just a plastic ball that I could play with along with my friends. To be honest, most of the boys my age who I ran with, would also get a ball.

And so it would be that we would take to the streets in our bare feet, mark out goals with a set of stones and just play and play and play.

That was possibly one of the advantages of a lack of private transport – you could play quite safely in the streets, particularly throughout the summer.

I say the streets.

They were, in fact, soil tracks, laced throughout the city.

The soil.

To stand on the soil, in one's bare feet, was to commune with nature and God.

We came from the soil, and we would return to the soil – that is what I believe.

I doubt there was ever a day during those long months when I wasn't kicking a ball.

The ball.

So important as they were not easy to get so, as I say, the New Year's Eve present was treated like the most precious commodity on earth.

When the inevitable happened and we burst the cheap plastic, we would take the ball to a man who repaired bicycles and he would use a tyre puncture kit, administer a patch over the hole, reinflate the ball with a pump and we could keep on playing.

He would not have known, of course, that he was restoring life to a ball for a boy who would go on to captain his country on the world stage – but that would be in another time.

I remember a moment when my constant kicking of a ball, playing one-twos with myself off my neighbour's wall, had disastrous results when, for the umpteenth occasion, a high clearance had gone into his backyard too often.

As I waited for the ball to be thrown back it arrived, stabbed through the heart by a kitchen knife and devoid of all life.

Once again, it was bicycle repair shop time!

We lived on the streets during those summer months. There was no better place to be, and we were either playing football or maybe, spending our time fencing with wooden swords.

Again, you would find someone who was good at woodwork and have them fashion a small sword for you and a few for your friends.

As I said before, I look back at my childhood with happiness. They were simple times, and our pleasures were easy.

As a child, you could not understand the concept of anti-materialism espoused by the dictatorship. It was just how it was, and you were a part of the system. You were educated, moulded by that system.

The theory was very simple.

We were taught that Albania was the most beautiful country in the world, and we were to be the happiest people on the planet.

My first school was called Vasil Shanto. Once again, it was named after a Partisan hero who had been killed in the war as was my secondary school, Xheladin Fishta.

If you visit Shkoder now, you will be struck by the fact that the schools, hospitals, prisons and state offices were all designed along the same lines.

Soulless concrete structures – corridors, bland walls – a feeling of being trapped in a colourless environment. That was the legacy of the communist times and their sterile architects.

On a recent visit to Xheladin Fishta, on a reconnaissance trip for this book, my co-writer Gerard McDade and I were allowed to look around my old school.

It had been some 30 years since I had walked these corridors and there were powerful moments of nostalgia as we did so.

One of the things that struck Gerard forcibly was the toilets.

We recall them as Turkish toilets which, in essence, was a hole in the ground. Whereas, in the West, lavatories are places where one can sit down on an actual seat, contemplate the world and go about one's personal ablutions, that was not the case where I was brought up.

Toilet bowls were flat and flush with the floor.

For the sake of decency, I will refrain from explaining the gymnastics involved; it is enough to simply understand that was the case.

Indeed, many years later when my wife, Annfrances and I were on a visit to my hometown and in the house of a good friend, she excused herself to go to the toilet.

She told me later, there was no toilet, but a hole in the ground, surrounded by porcelain.

I was left to explain the situation. Anyway ...

Sport was heavily encouraged throughout the education process.

Communists always saw sport as a healthy recreation but one that took the mind away from other thoughts.

When I was growing up in Shkoder, I didn't have to be asked twice to get involved in playing a game.

I enjoyed school, given that I was naturally active and, even now, thirsty for knowledge. Both Shanto and Fishta were geared towards identifying specific talents and skills in fields such as sport and music.

I graduated to secondary school when I was ten.

Education in Albania at that time? Politics, pure and simple.

We were taught the teachings of the great figures of communist history right up to Enver Hoxha who, of course, believed *himself* to be a great figure in that history.

Karl Marx. Joseph Stalin. Vladimir Lenin. Friedrich Engels.

All these leaders and philosophers constituted the essential core of our school curriculum.

Yes, there was room for the sciences such as chemistry, physics, biology and mathematics, but at the heart of our education was communist ideology.

In time, I would come to reject this form of brainwashing and try to discover a philosophy of my own which, to be honest, had the potential to completely wreck my future but that was further down the line.

For the moment, I was looking to get to a secondary school that would allow me to continue my education and just play football.

The way it worked was that professional coaches from Fishta would come down to our primary school and they would run a series of trials to identify those boys who were considered good enough to enter their school.

The trials went well for me so I was asked if I was interested in attending Fishta and, I have to say, I was very happy to go there.

I would see out my early education but with a view to developing my talent for football.

As I mentioned earlier, volleyball was Aleks' game, and he went to a different school to follow that course.

There was less of a structure to school football, but I got to play a lot and felt that I was nurturing my range of skills.

In those early years, I was a a centre-forward and, naturally, was amongst the goals. It's hard to believe now, but we would sometimes train five times a week, all of the sessions lasting over 90 minutes.

It honed your talents as well as developing your athleticism and physique.

When I was 13, we played in an invitational tournament, and this was my first real experience of competitive football.

We lived in the north region and so we battled it out with other sides and the winners would take on the successful team from the south region.

The eventual winners were Tirana and we finished second to them which, given that they were a city team with heavier resources and linked to 'the Party', was quite an achievement. It gave great credit to us.

On a personal level, I had a very successful competition, scoring goals for fun and, in fact, finishing as the top goal scorer in the tournament.

This led to my name being put out a lot in one of the big sports newspapers at the time which, naturally, led to interest in my potential growth from some professional clubs.

When I turned 14, I left secondary school, as was the custom in Albania.

I now had to look to further education and that path could potentially lie before me in the Albanian capital, Tirana, at the Loro Borici school.

Borici was, possibly in his day, the most respected footballer in Albania.

His playing career, which had started in 1937 when he was only 15, had seen him turn out for my local side Vllaznia Shkodër before signing for SS Lazio in 1941.

He spent two years at the Italian side before returning to his homeland and Shkoder again where he captained the team to two league titles.

It was a similar story of success when he moved to Partizani Tirana in 1949, where he once again picked up championships.

Moving into management with Partizani, he led the club to three league titles and four cups.

Having represented his country as a player, he went on to manage the national team over a remarkable five periods.

His name was an Albanian byword for football integrity as he devoted his entire life to the game. I don't believe he ever married, just stayed loyal to football.

Consequently, entry to the Loro Borici school was not only viewed as a potential step to a career in the game, but it was also a considerable honour and their remit was to produce the Albanian stars of the future. In effect, the *next* Borici!

Here was a seat of education that not only had subjects such as physics, maths, chemistry and anatomy on the curriculum, but also taught the history of world football, charting the stories of World Cup tournaments and European campaigns as well as exploring the big names and legends of the game.

My schooling in Shkoder had provided the ABC of the game, but if I could get into Borici, I could complete my X, Y and Z.

The top scouts from the school had seen me play in tournaments. I was invited to trials in Tirana and was so pleased when I was offered a place at Loro Borici.

It meant, of course that, at 14, I was leaving my family to go to Tirana.

I look back at it now and realise how young I was to be taking this on, but at that time, it felt like the most normal decision in the world.

However, life away from home, away from my family was incredibly tough.

I actually felt like an orphan.

First of all, there was the journey to Tirana itself.

This involved a three-hour train ride in the worst of facilities.

In years to come, I would marvel at the luxury and comfort of a modern footballer at a big club like Celtic as we moved around Scotland and Europe to play our football.

Everything was the best. All our requirements were catered for, and we were cosseted from place to place by a team of administrators who made sure we were able to travel without any hindrance so that we were able to channel our energies into winning matches.

At Celtic, every detail, from your passport to tickets, to accommodation were taken care of by Therese Cassidy, who did a marvellous job of ensuring your transit was of the highest quality and efficiently taken care of on behalf of the club.

The focus was simple. We do *our* job; you do *your* job.

And that was back in the 1990s. I imagine it has evolved way beyond that in this day and age.

When I was 14, that three-hour train journey to Tirana was on a par with animals being taken in steerage across the country.

Equally, the living facilities at Loro Borici were, at best, deliberately crude.

Essentially, the school had converted army barracks into dormitories with the most basic living conditions imaginable.

The only shower facilities were actually in the school, so you had to go there in the morning for a proper wash.

Outside of that, there was, effectively, a trough in the barracks where you could get a basic wash to get you ready for the day.

We ate in a communal canteen and the diet was meagre, to say the least. Like all schools, of course, Borici had its fair share of bullying, older boys who got a sadistic pleasure out of the treatment of their juniors.

They would generally be around 17 or 18 years of age and seemed to have the power to make life hell for the younger boys.

They delighted in their demands that, for example, you had to wash their clothes for them and endure regular beatings.

You had to stand up to them, which was never easy, and I was on the end of a few batterings myself.

I would, however, plot my revenge and find a way of hitting back at one or two of them when nobody was looking.

That felt particularly sweet and totally justified.

Those first few months at Borici were extremely tough and I am not ashamed to say that I regularly cried myself to sleep, but I knew that returning home was not an option even though I seriously missed my family.

This was the new course of my life and I had to strengthen myself for the road ahead.

Fron an early age, I had to develop a mental toughness, and this was my education in how that had to be.

Besides, I considered myself privileged to be given this opportunity and because at that stage I was an under-15 international, my parents did not have to pay for me to attend Loro Borici.

In addition, although the food was bland and monotonous, I was also entitled to extra rations as a member of the international set-up, so I wasn't being short-changed on that front either.

The training and conditioning were intense, and we were under the charge of a coach named Aurel Verria.

He was a remarkable man and, even at that stage of my life, a powerful and enduring influence.

Coach Verria believed in discipline, mental toughness and supreme physical fitness, and in the pre-season he worked us hard.

Yes, football was about tactics, but if you were not fit enough to play then those tactics would be irrelevant.

He would take us into the gym, order us down on to the floor and insist upon ten push-ups from each of us.

Incredibly, as we all complied, and there would be about 20 of us, he would stand and mentally count out the push-ups of every boy. He asked me, one day, how many I had done, and I replied, *'13'*.

He knew that I had and asked me why I had done more than I was asked, and I told him that I felt a few of them weren't of the required standard so I did a few more.

He liked that answer and then turned to another boy and asked him the same question to which the answer came back, 'ten'.

Coach Verria looked at the boy and then addressed him, *No. You only did eight, because two of them were not up to standard. Rudi has done more because he understands that if you do not do the exercise properly, then you must compensate for it.*

This dedicated man was giving me the right ingredients to better myself. He kept me right, believed in me and made me captain of the team.

I was learning lessons for life and, even now, some 40 years later, I can still recall the influence of coach Aurel Verria.

I had one good friend at this time and his name was Blenard Hasami.

We bonded over football, of course, although Blenard wasn't the most talented of players. But he had the heart of a lion and I always believe that every team needs a player like that in their ranks.

Together, we enjoyed our football, formed a close relationship and this was our guard against the bullyboys of Loro Borici school. We looked out for each other throughout our time in school.

It was a friendship that endured up until Blenard's untimely death in 1998.

Our survival instincts helped us to get by any way we could, and, in my friend's case, that meant, ultimately, dealing in illegal contraband.

At that point, some seven years after the collapse of communism, crime, gangsters and guns were the currency of the time and Blenard had got himself involved to the point where he was gunned down in the streets of Berat – a major city in the south of Albania.

This period was akin to a civil war.

Perhaps I have to thank football for keeping me off that path as the course of one's life can change dramatically based upon the cards one is dealt.

When I was at Loro Borici, the capital city of Albania was also host to three of the biggest clubs in the country – Partizani Tirana, Dinamo Tirana and KF Tirana.

To truly understand the politics in Albania then, it is important to know the sporting history of these clubs.

KF were founded in 1920 and are universally recognised as the most successful team in the country with over 50 major domestic trophies to their name. I would say that they were the benchmark for any team in the country and, up until the Second World War, they enjoyed a rivalry with my hometown team, which, as mentioned before, is Vllaznia Shkoder.

However, please note the date the club were inaugurated, 1920, and the expression, '… up until the Second World War'.

As I have stated before, the aftermath of the war changed everything in Albania – even the football.

Communism, the party system, the forces of law, order and military observance were now under the auspices of government and that included sport.

Under Enver Hoxha, the Party insisted, first of all, that KF Tirana changed the name of the club to *17 Nentori,* literally 17 November.

This was in commemoration of the liberation of Tirana on that date in 1944.

The club, naturally, were left with no option but to comply with this order as the alternative was expulsion, but further suffering was handed out when, in 1946, FK Partizani were founded to offer rivalry to the Nentori.

Partizani were a football club affiliated to the army. In other words, the Defence Ministry, a significant branch of the government.

Officially, they produced players who had served in the military, and most were recruited from the Albanian Military Academy or the Skanderbeg Military High School.

Unofficially, the ruling communists in the Politburo ordered other players to leave their clubs and sign for Partizani.

Naturally, with such an influx of talent, this led to the club winning their first national title in their inaugural season and with players of the calibre of the great Loro Borici in the team, they would enjoy a period of domination during those early years.

In 1950, the Ministry of the Interior, effectively the police in Albania, having watched the success of the army side, decided to form a club, Dinamo Tirana, as a representation of the 'law and order' branch of the Politburo.

The new club were successful immediately, going on to win consecutive national championships from inception in 1950 to 1953.

Politics, having been invasive in every part of the social and cultural components of Albanian society, had now flexed its considerable Politburo muscles in the sporting arena.

The net result was the squeezing out of 17 Nentori and the emergence of Partizani and Dinamo as the Celtic and Rangers of the Albanian game.

Nentori, remarkably, stayed resilient and were finally rewarded in 1964 when, under charismatic manager and former KF player Myslym Alla, the club won their first national title in 20 years. They repeated the feat the following season, but it was not a development that would go unnoticed in the corridors of power patrolled by the army generals of Partizani and the secret service forces at Dinamo.

In June of 1967, Partizani and Nentori contested a league match towards the end of the campaign when a fight broke out among the players. The scenes were described as 'disgraceful' and the match was abandoned.

Both clubs were ordered to forfeit the game 0-3, were deducted three points and also told to lose, by default, their remaining three games of the season.

It meant that Dinamo would automatically claim the title over Nentori.

This was the 'decision' of the Albanian Football Federation, but it appeared to be one taken in collaboration with the all-powerful Politburo.

Certainly, UEFA must have come to that conclusion as, after a report into the affair, they never officially recognised that particular championship campaign.

This, then, gives you some idea of the football scene in the country with the national capital at the heart of it all.

Football had the dark forces of the Communist Party pulling the strings and one thing was certain – it did not matter how good a player you were; you would never be allowed to pursue a professional career outside Albania.

To consider it was inconceivable.

And, to ever share the ambition of it with anyone else was to leave you, and possibly your family, open to being arrested and put in prison.

More of that later.

* * *

When I was 18, I had to pursue a career path.

Of course, I wanted to play football but that would not have been enough to fund a better lifestyle for myself in the future.

My realistic goal at that point in my life was to go to a sports university and train to be a PE teacher.

With a degree such as that, I would also be able to look at coaching as a potential outlet for me.

And yet, my football was continuing to develop, which leads me to the next key moment in my life which began this chapter.

That was when I accompanied the Albanian under-18 squad to Holland for a trip that would stir my soul and foment my imagination.

CHAPTER 5

# THE SIGNATURE

The trip to Holland had ignited something in me.

Perhaps it took me back to watching that great Netherlands side of 1974 and Ruud Krol.

For the first time I saw the world of the West and it seemed to represent one thing – freedom.

This was not a word to be taken lightly, especially to my parents' generation who had lived the greater parts of their lives under oppression and dictatorship.

The official dogma was to be born, live and die in Albania.

To consider otherwise was deemed unthinkable and my parents understood that. However, when Aleks and I were young, my father took a radical step that, possibly, showed us that he could see a different future for us.

Albanian was the mother tongue and to speak another language was completely outlawed, but my father decided that my brother and I should arm ourselves for the future by learning Italian.

This was an incredibly incendiary decision, fraught with genuine danger on the part of my father. Had he been caught then at the very least, he would have been sent to prison, but worse even than that, potentially despatched to a gulag.

It wasn't just the actual teaching of the language, which was punishable enough in itself: it was the subterfuge involved in which he smuggled a Catholic priest into the house after dark. I called him *Uncle Ndreka*, who, incidentally, had been persecuted in jail for more than 20 years.

The period from 1946 right up until 1990/91 was riven with the persecution of Catholic priests by the communist authorities in my homeland. From an estimated 70 Franciscan Fathers in the country, a mere nine would survive the purge against the church.

In Shkoder today we have the *Librari At Gjergi Fishta,* dedicated to the Franciscan Fathers and a constant reminder of the sacrifices these men made for their faith and their country.

Padre Gjergi Fishta was a remarkable and revered man.

A friar, writer, poet and educator, he became one of the most influential and cultural figures in Albanian history.

He had a passion for the country and the people and involved himself in the political life of Albania at a time of great change in the first half of the 20th century.

He represented our country at the Conference of Versailles in the post-war period of 1919 and went on to become deputy chairman of the Albanian parliament in the early 1920s.

After campaigning for his preferred and ultimately unsuccessful candidate to lead that parliament and the country in 1924, he voluntarily put himself in to exile in Italy in 1925, where he passed away 15 years later.

Such was his influence that, even six years after his death and the emergence of the dictator, Enver Hoxha, his writings, teachings and texts were expunged from Albanian public life.

The communists considered him a threat – even from the grave.

Consequently, as a child and even as an adult, I was unaware of his name or his magnitude.

It was only later, as an adult, that I came to understand this man and his prestigious place in the story of my country.

This was the tangible danger of having anything to do with religion, politics or the church for any ordinary Albanian.

The penalty for Uncle Ndreka, had he been discovered, would have been considerable for both him and my father.

The cleric accepted that risk and so he would sit with us down in the cellar and educate us by candlelight.

The risk was substantial, and I will never, ever, forget the sacrifice that both my father and Uncle Ndreka were willing to make so that Aleks and I could have a future.

Not surprisingly, given the potential dangers, we were determined not to let my father down and eagerly devoured the language.

However, by 1987, I was ready for the next step in my development and the plates of life were shifting to present an opportunity.

Muhedin (Mujo) Targaj was the revered and charismatic captain of Dinamo Tirana.

The definition of a one-club man, he had won five league titles and a couple of cups with the club in his time but had announced that he was retiring in that summer of 1987.

I was fortunate enough to have been seen playing in that under-18 tournament against the best of Dutch youth, when I operated at centre-back, Mujo's position.

The powers that be at Dinamo had seen me and decided that I had the potential to be the natural replacement for the talismanic Targaj.

This was an astonishing vote of confidence in me given my relative inexperience at a high level, and the decision had been taken to sign me for the club.

However, this being Albania, my pathway to Dinamo was to prove a very convoluted one.

Having completed my education, the natural expectation was that I would return to my hometown of Shkoder and play for Vllaznia.

I was happy to do so, but there now took place a series of events that, at the very least, threatened to torpedo my future career in the game and, at the very worst, affect me and my family with the most horrific of outcomes.

It appeared that, for some reason, my father was being linked with spying for the Yugoslavian authorities.

It was outrageous, an outright lie, and above all, an incredibly dangerous suggestion.

How had this accusation come about?

I have no idea, but in those dark days, all it took was one letter to the authorities from an outraged individual and, based on gossip or hearsay, you would be investigated as my father was by the state.

The *Sigurimi* were still very much at large in the country.

Who is to say why such an accusation could be lodged and the worst accusation of all – an anonymous one?

As my poor father sought to deal with it, and the potential fallout, I found myself embroiled in a situation brought about by my first European adventure with Vllaznia Shkoder.

By winning the Albanian Cup, Vllaznia had qualified to compete in the European Cup Winnerss' Cup competition for 1987/88 and I was a part of the squad.

In the first round we were drawn to play against Sliema Wanderers of Malta, and, in a match I felt we dominated, we won 2-0 in front of an enthusiastic support.

The second leg, out in Malta, would be no formality, but in fine form, we triumphed 4-0. That was impressive. Six goals over two games with no reply and a terrific team performance away from home.

The trip back to Albania was broken up by a stopover in Rome. An overnight stay and a chance to relax in the confines of a decent hotel in the Italian capital.

It was my first experience of this beautiful city.

I was certainly relaxed, young and enjoying life at the time.

Courtesy of Uncle Ndreka, my Italian was almost fluent and so, unlike my team-mates, I was comfortable in the surroundings of the city and the ability to converse with the natives – especially the waiters who looked after us at the hotel.

This was also the first time I had experienced Coca-Cola.

Coke represented the ultimate example of American imperialism to the communists of Albania.

A soft drink that had become a corporate giant, a market leader all across the globe, sold on the thirst of nations who would not just be enjoying a soft drink but imbibing the freedoms in Albania.

It was of little surprise, therefore, that the drink was banned throughout my home country.

I was 18 years of age and was about to taste it for the first time.

The sugar was an instant hit and, lying back at the hotel swimming pool, perhaps with the natural adrenaline of youth, the imminent feeling of adulthood and the rush of the sugar, I found myself on a natural high.

The ability to talk in Italian to the locals was enjoyable, but perhaps, in a way, I showed my hand too much.

By my very conversation, I was admitting that I was fluent in a language other than Albanian.

It was when one of my team-mates, Faslli Fakja suggested, with a smile, that I could stay in Rome and adapt to the Italian lifestyle very easily, that my troubles began.

Such an innocent statement, but in Albanian terms, absolute dynamite.

I honestly cannot remember if I replied in the affirmative, but it would not have mattered anyway.

Someone, somewhere, had logged the notion that I was conversant in a foreign tongue, was open to moving to another country, another way of life, even though I am certain that I had said no such thing.

Who is to say how they came about this information? It certainly had not come from Faslli, whom I trusted completely and who remains a friend to this day.

The *Sigurimi* were everywhere – eyes and ears. Anything was possible.

In the next round, Vllaznia were drawn against FK RoPS of Finland.

Ultimately, this tie would be a defining moment in Albanian football.

In Shkoder, we conceded a goal midway through the first half and lost the match 1-0, but we felt we were not out of the tie of course and prepared for the second leg.

It was a match in which myself and Faslli would not take part, however, as my friend was told that he would not be travelling to the airport.

Me?

I was allowed on the bus, but for some reason, was not allowed on to the aeroplane and so I returned to my hometown.

There was now a problem – a *serious* problem.

I had been identified as someone with potential ambition.

The second leg of the tie resulted in a 1-0 defeat for the team, and we were out of the competition, but that was the most remote issue to me.

On the way back from the game and, in the course of a stopover in Athens, two of the Vllaznia players, Arvid Hoxha (no relation to Enver) and Lulezhim (Luli) Bershemi, defected, seeking political asylum.

This was now a matter of state – and the state reacted quickly.

When the rest of the now depleted squad returned to Shkoder, there was an immediate inquest by the party resulting in a meeting with us all in a local hotel, the Rozafa – a mere 500 yards from my own front door. The secretary of the Party had been summoned and it was he who addressed us.

He was explicit in both his condemnation and the consequences of the actions of Hoxha and Bershemi.

I recall that he spat out the word *traitors* on numerous occasions.

They were, in his words, enemies of their country – the country that had nourished, raised and provided for their respective families and now the fate of their actions would resound as thunder down upon those families.

Chillingly, he deliberately chose not to tell us the nature of that fate, but rather left it hanging in the wind, allowing our minds to conjure up all sorts of scenarios – and none of them pleasant.

Banishment to the mountains was the very least punishment they could expect as, in turn, it appeared to be the case for one of the coaches of the team and some of the backroom staff who had allowed this to happen on their watch.

Indeed, in due course, they were removed from their positions and forced to lose any privileges by being banished into the iniquity of the hills.

This was a rugged, mountainous region that only heavy-duty lorries could access and there they would live out the rest of their lives by instructing children in sports and other educational activities without seeing their families.

It was as we were digesting these frightening thoughts that the secretary's attention was drawn to another matter.

A more sinister matter for me, as it would appear.

Out of nowhere, he announced that they knew that there was *another* traitor in the room. He let it linger again, but I was in no doubt that he was referring to Rudi Vata.

It was now a period of great concern for both me and my family. I could make a case for saying that I had never referred in any way to relocating to Rome.

My father could declare his innocence to any charges, but this was Albania in 1987: there was no right of appeal. No way to clarify a position when there appeared to be evidence, *anonymous* evidence that could bring the wrath of the Party down upon the Vata family.

My future – and the immediate future of my father, mother and brother – lay in the caprices of a dogmatic, vicious Party apparatus. Little could I have known that all of our fates lay in the evolving consequences of the retirement of Muhedin Targaj as the first-choice centre-half of Dinamo Tirana.

A man named Hekuran Isai was not just the director of the club, he was also the Minister of the Interior, head of the hated *Sigurimi,* and, at that time, one of the most powerful individuals in the country: perhaps second only to Prime Minister Adil Carcani in that respect.

Sport was a passion for him and, it appeared, his goal was to drive Dinamo Tirana to the pinnacle of Albanian domestic football with potential European participation as well.

One day, I was urged to travel to Tirana and call into his office at the Dinamo stadium.

I say *urged*, but when the second-most powerful man in the country wants to speak to you face-to-face, it was not a request – it was an order.

I complied immediately, travelled through to the capital and entered his office.

As I stood there, taking in the man who held the power over my family and me, there was no room to breathe.

The accusations against my father were as ridiculous as they were false. The suggestion that I was about to embark on a football career and a life in Italy were equally so, but none of that mattered.

At the time, he referenced lengthy correspondence that was lying on his desk and was relevant to my father as well as myself.

How was I to know if he was playing out some outrageous bluff? I was never going to be allowed to see this correspondence or paperwork. For all I knew, it could have been his shopping list!

Yet. There he sat, like a modern-day Caesar, with the absolute power to put his thumb up … or down … on the life of me and my family.

He spelt it out.

There was trouble for my family … information had been shown to him … anonymous letters suggested very strongly … it could be difficult to refute or resolve this …

For my part, all I could do was stand there and listen to this without recourse to stating the case for myself and my father.

In my head, I could imagine the fates that awaited us.

The mountains.

The gulags.

Banishment forever.

And yet, oddly, I felt a certain relaxation.

One often hears that, in one's final seconds, a peace descends upon one and eases the transition from life to death.

Why would he be telling me all of this?

What was his motivation?

Was it simply a power play before, symbolically, decapitating me and my family?

The answer became clear to me when he looked at me and announced abruptly that he wanted me to commit myself to Dinamo Tirana.

He saw me as an integral future part of the club and had faith in me to deliver on and off the park.

And now I saw it all in front of me.

All the so-called *evidence* against my father.

All the ludicrous suggestions that I had aspirations to leave the country and hand my family over to the fates of the *Sigurimi.*

All the politics, subterfuge, jealousy, call it what you will – all of it led up to this moment.

Hekuran Isai was either my saviour or my crucifier – and *only* he.

The man was prepared to simply sign a letter to the effect that there was no substance to all of the allegations stacked against me and my father.

He would do it now – if I pledged myself to his football club, the team of the Ministry of the Interior.

My ability out on a football pitch, my commitment to Dinamo Tirana, these were the differences between destruction and salvation.

*That* was Albania in 1987.

The letter he signed – a piece of paper bearing the signature on it of potentially the second-most powerful man in Albania – was the difference for me, my family and our future.

My life; my career; my move to Scotland that resulted in me meeting my life partner; the raising of our two sons; the chance for the freedom that I cherished more than anyone else in any football dressing room that I would ever go on to occupy – all of that lay in the signature of a powerful man in the summer of 1987.

One man.

The capriciousness of life.

Fate?

A trust in God that your life could be guided?

Who is to say?

All I know is that everything that was to follow, the journey I was on, the potential longevity of my parents' lives together, lay in a signature on a piece of paper.

And, in front of me, he signed that paper.

How was that for *real* power?

## CHAPTER 6

# BLUE SUBMARINE

And yet, was it *real* power, as such?

There was an occasion shortly after I became a Dinamo Tirana player that did make me wonder about the shadow of Hekuran Isai.

An occasion that seemed to show the fragility of men like him who jockeyed for power and influence, knowing that they would have to trample upon people to get it whilst, equally, leaving themselves open to becoming vulnerable themselves.

The truth of the matter was that I never actually signed for Dinamo Tirana in 1987. There was no formal contract offered; no signature on a dotted line as Celtic would come to discover in 1992 when they wanted to bring me to Glasgow.

Instead, you entered a system, a way of life, rather than a football club.

Though young, I was not naive.

I knew that Dinamo was the creature of the Ministry of the Interior – that politics gave birth to the club and sustained it throughout its lifetime.

You were not necessarily playing for a team; you were part of a departmental political rivalry between two of the most powerful branches of the dictatorial regime – the army and the police.

By 1987, Enver Hoxha was dead, having succumbed to diabetes two years previously, but the oppressive machine that he had put into place with all its secrecy, subterfuge and corruption was still in force.

The head had been cut off, but the body somehow remained intact. Under his leadership, Albania had become possibly the most isolated country in the world.

Changes were in the wind, but in that summer of 1987, I could not see them. I do not believe *anyone* could see them!

The system dictated that I returned to the town of my birth as they had a local professional club, and that I should play for them, but then the politics took over.

Yes, I should remain at Vllaznia, but now one of the government teams wanted me and so they cleared a path to make it possible – much to the annoyance and, possibly, the jealousy of the Vllaznia officials, who could not compete with that level of autocracy. The Ministry of the Interior had wielded their considerable power.

Listen, I was 18 years of age and embarking on the career that I had always dared to dream of – that of a professional footballer. If that meant going to Tirana to fulfil my destiny, then so be it.

Dinamo Tirana was a good club. They had a stringent approach to discipline and insisted that we all lived at the ground.

Imagine that.

Imagine saying to Henrik Larsson, 'Welcome to Celtic. We have a bunk ready for you at the back of the main stand!'

It was, however, a question of perspective. I never queried the fact that we lived out in the stadium, I just accepted it as a matter of course.

Perhaps, in a sense, it bonded us as a team.

Our lifestyle was simple anyway. As a group, we socialised together, but let's be honest, at that time there weren't really any clubs, bars or discotheques in Tirana.

If you wanted a beer, then you visited a restaurant and had a meal.

You didn't even need to go out for that meal. There was a restaurant out at the ground, and you had your own room complete with a bed and a television. I had no complaints. This was the path I had chosen and the route I wanted to go down.

The club were also allowing me to continue with my education so that I could complete my all-important sports degree.

On Monday, I attended the college.

Tuesday to Friday was devoted to training, conditioning the body with a total focus on what was to come at the weekend – the match which was either played on a Saturday or a Sunday.

There was no actual salary at the club.

Officially, you were on 1,500 Albanian Lek per month, but you never saw it, as it catered for your bed and board and there was little point in asking about it.

In comparison, my father would have been taking home around 7,000 Lek per month.

Hekuran Isai was always around the club, hanging out with the players, challenging them to table tennis matches.

He seemed to like the camaraderie, or perhaps he was just looking to escape the constant back-stabbing that was the story of political life in the country.

Politically, it was good to let him win on the table, but I was not built that way and so I gave it my all, beating him on a regular basis.

His bodyguards would stand around, expressionless save for their eyes scrutinising every movement, with their arms folded, guarding their political master as I trounced him on the table.

*Whoa, Rudi! Let him win a few games, please!!* my team-mates would say to me, but what was the point of playing a game unless you were prepared to give it everything?

I actually think our CEO respected that fact and me, for that matter. I am not saying he took defeat well, but I did feel he awarded me a certain status.

He had seen something in me.

A talent perhaps, out on the football field, but maybe even an attitude that would serve me well with him.

However, then came that moment when I could see the potential fragility of his own position and his place in the system that had moulded him.

In the early days of my time as a Dinamo Tirana player, the club were due to fly over to Turkey for a Balkan Cup match.

I was looking forward to my first trip away as a professional footballer, but Hekuran Isai was taking a slightly different view of proceedings.

He took me aside one day, on my own, and revealed to me his thoughts.

Effectively, he told me that he had gone into bat for me – that his signature had not only provided a potential career for me but also relieved my family of a certain fate.

There had been an incident when some players from another club had gone to Turkey for a match only for them to defect and seek political asylum in Athens, Greece.

He asked for my guarantee, my *absolute* guarantee that I would not contemplate such an action.

Not only would such a course be fatal for my family, but it would also have the direst repercussions on *him* as my guarantor.

He would unquestionably have been sent to prison himself, an outcast from the Party and political life forever more.

Here, now, was a strange situation – an about-face, if you like.

Hekuran Isai had guaranteed the immediate future of my life and the lives of my family and yet, for all that, I was in a position of power myself in respect of his own situation.

To be honest, there was no question of my defection at that point, in any case.

I knew the consequences for my family of such an action.

Later on, I would have contact from an unofficial Albanian agent suggesting that the powerful Swedish side, IFK Gothenburg, wanted to take me on as a player and, tempted as I was, it was a complete non-starter.

My family would suffer as a consequence and that, to me, was the ultimate act of betrayal to the people who had cared for me, raised me and made me the man I was to become.

I gave Hekuran Isai my word that I would make no attempt to jump ship and seek political asylum.

He eyed me suspiciously, but I was then, and remain now, a man of my word. When I give that word and shake your hand, you can take it to the bank.

And so, my education began at Dinamo Tirana or, as they were nicknamed by the support, the *Blue Submarine* due to the colour of our strips. I joined the club in October, and they had not started the season well.

It had only been two years since they were champions of the *Kategoria Superiore*, the Albanian top division, but this would be a struggling campaign for the club.

The reason for this slump in form? Who can say?

Perhaps there was a sense of transition around the place. In fact, when Dinamo first expressed their interest in me as a potential player, it was under the auspices of manager Fatmir Frasheri. He was a respected man in the game and had been Albanian national manager in the 1960s, but as ever, the politics around the club orchestrated a move to remove him from his position.

When I arrived in the October, a new man was in charge – Bejkush Birce. He, of course, as you know from previous chapters, would go on to become national manager as well and, in fact, as you may recall, would be the man to give me my first cap as well as shake my hand and wish me well that night in Paris when I left the Concorde Montparnasse hotel, looking for my freedom.

We had an excellent working relationship and personally got on really well into the bargain.

He identified qualities in me and knew that, even at 18, I was not inhibited in any way by the task ahead of fitting into a top-flight club.

He encouraged me in our training sessions and regularly pitted me against one of the Dinamo and Albanian legends in our country – the formidable midfielder, Sulejman Demollari.

Five years older than me and a player who, after the fall of communism, would go on to be considered one of the best foreigners to play in Romania with Dinamo Bucharest, Sulejman was a lynchpin in our side.

He was the architect of previous club successes – an assured, confident footballer, who played with grit and grace.

Birce was more than happy, however, for me to go one v one with Sulejman in training.

This was one of many ways that I was learning the game and, crucially, growing up in the process.

Our manager was ultimately looking to combine youth with experience in what his image of what Dinamo should be in the future, but, in my first season, we were yet to see the fruits of that vision.

There was no question that we were struggling throughout that campaign, losing marginally more games than we won and certainly drawing too many matches.

Our final position for the season was 11th out of 14, but in reality, only two points separated us from the automatic relegation berth occupied by city of Berat-based side, KF Tomori, so it was a close-run thing.

After the complication of the relegation rounds, we were down to play a two-leg play-off against the runners-up in the second tier, Naftetari Qyteti Stalin which, as their name suggests, were a side who had strong communist links.

The tie went on to become one of the most notorious in the history of Albanian sport.

The first leg was on our home ground and, although the 1-0 scoreline sounds narrow, I felt we had been reasonably comfortable throughout the match.

The return leg was in Qyteti Stalin on 5 June 1988.

A 1-0 lead, of course, was always perilous and the hostility that we felt from the home support that afternoon was genuine.

By now, the pressure on us was immense. Throughout their 38 years of history, FK Dinamo Tirana had never been relegated to a lower division, so we were acutely aware of what was at stake that day. It was a tense encounter that always threatened to boil over, and it did at full time after we had won 1-0, courtesy of an Arben Vila goal, for a 2-0 aggregate victory.

Afterwards, there was a suggestion that the fact that the match officials all came from Tirana was a factor in what took place, but to be honest, I have to dismiss that theory.

We were, quite simply, the better side over the two legs.

The referee and his assistants all had the required credentials and badges to officiate in the match, but I suppose, if you were looking for a conspiracy theory, there it was!

Anyway, on full time, the crowd invaded the pitch in huge numbers, and it became clear that they had only one idea in mind – to exact physical revenge upon our team!

In fact, they looked as if they wanted to kill us!

Somehow, we were shepherded into the relative safety of the away dressing room with a strict line of security outside the door, formed by the local police.

Presumably, they were under the orders of the Ministry of the Interior to look after the 'police' team.

Outside, you could hear the venom and rancour raining down on us and the advice from the police was that we were to sit tight until they could restore order.

But, hey, Rudi was 19 – young, headstrong and with the blood in his body at a heightened level.

It could have been the adrenaline, of course, but I got outside and stood shouting at the mob.

If they wanted a fight, then I was the one to give it.

Perhaps it was my age, but I loved the situation. For once, the freedom to cut loose, raise a voice in anger, make a challenge – it felt empowering. That was something that you did not get to experience as an Albanian at that time.

In the middle of it all, astonishingly, I suddenly caught sight of my friend from my first days at Loro Borici school in Tirana, Blenard Hasami.

Typically, for a man with the heart of a lion, he was right at the core of the action giving as good as he got. Blenard Hasami was never a guy for half measures.

I am not sure the police knew what to make of it, but just as quickly as I got out, I was dragged back in to the dressing room.

Things were now taking an even uglier turn as we were told that the rioters had taken over our team bus and had set fire to it.

It was a burning, hollowed-out mess, and the word now was that special forces were on their way from Tirana itself to help us.

They would have been the Albanian equivalent of the US Marines, or the British SAS and they were accompanying a substitute bus to take us back home.

What a time it was that we had to wait, and, in those days, there were no mobile phones or computers to tell us all what was happening.

Equally, it was still the Albania of communism and Party power so we would have been left ignorant and in the dark anyway.

It was late at night before we were escorted into the streets of Qyteti Stalin and put on to the substitute bus.

We were tired, physically drained and hungry, but relieved to finally get out of town and on the two-hour drive to Tirana.

The aftermath of this uprising and rioting was merciless on FK Naftetari as they were suspended from playing football for a year and demoted to the third-tier division.

In addition, for their conduct throughout the affair, club coach Pandi Angjeli and players Meta and Makashi were suspended for life whilst manager Fatmir Ismaili was removed from his role.

Any way that I looked at it, this had been quite an introductory season for Rudi Vata as a professional player. What an experience!

* * *

The following season of 1988/89 could not be allowed to come down to a relegation play-off fight for Dinamo Tirana and Bejkush Birce knew that, so he set about working on the upcoming campaign.

He made subtle changes to the squad and worked us hard out on the training ground.

In came experienced midfielder Viktor Briza from Vllaznia Shkoder and his impact was immediate both in the dressing room and out on the pitch.

Birce was now working on that blend of youth and experience that he believed in.

In my opinion, one of the best changes and, indeed, inspirational in a sense that the club was trying to move forward, was the investment in a new training complex down by the beautiful lakes of Tirana.

This was a statement of intent from the club and the facilities, by any standard, were first class.

There was a hotel, a restaurant and a gym. A feeling of real professionalism ran through the establishment and we, as players, responded to that professionalism.

For a start, we ran eventual title winners 17 Nentori close in the *Kategoria Superiore*. Just like the Scottish Premiership, Albania operated a split league system, except we did it long before Scotland followed suit.

The top six teams played each other in the final five weeks of the season, to see if they could add to their points tally and sort out the outcome of the title.

As a result, we went into the Top Six in third position and retained that until the end of the campaign.

It was a notable climb from the previous season and the last-day nerves of avoiding relegation for the first time in Dinamo's history.

Our football was good that year, and I knew that I was growing up with this team as a player and a man on a weekly basis.

Our greatest success that season, however, would lie in the *Kupa e Shqiperise*, the Albanian Cup.

The competition operated along the lines of the current European set-up in that there was a league for the opening games with four divisions and the top two teams from each going forward to the quarter-final stage.

Once there, we had an aggregate 5-2 victory over my hometown team, Vllaznia Shkoder, and I had to wonder if those petty jealousies of the officials who had tried to block my move to Dinamo in the first place had reached a real point of rage over the result. Were they raging against me or the system that had taken me from their club – who could say?

On to the semi-final and no harder draw than against the team who would be crowned *Kategoria Superiore* champions, the best in Albania for the season, 17 Nentori.

We worked hard for a 1-0 victory away from home before a tight 0-0 draw in Tirana saw us through to the final.

That would have been a highlight of the season, knocking the champions out of the cup, and waiting for us at that final hurdle was Partizani Tirana.

There would be so many factors in this one including the local rivalry of the two clubs from the same city, but additionally, Partizani had finished second that season in the league so, after 17 Nentori, there was no harder opponent on paper.

I was excited for my first domestic final as a professional player. Here, now, would be a measure of how far I had progressed in the game since my introduction to the top flight with Dinamo only 18 months previously.

I was 20 years of age, developing both mentally and physically, and now about to play in a national cup final.

Twenty thousand people, a sizeable crowd by Albanian standards, crammed into the Qeman Stafa Stadium in Tirana on 31 May 1989 for the showpiece occasion and climax of the season.

This would be the equivalent of Celtic v Rangers for the silverware and the passion from both sets of supporters would characterise the final.

It was one of those games of football when, perhaps, the fear of losing was the overriding factor as the sides produced a stalemate at 0-0.

The replay took place in the same stadium two days later and was a far better affair.

We had that classic early lead when full-back Eduard Abazi had us 1-0 up within four minutes.

I felt we were in control of the game but conceded an equaliser at the worst possible moment – within sight of half-time.

That would have given Partizani plenty of confidence so it was important we retained our composure at the break.

Bejkush Birce urged us to keep doing what we had been doing in the first half and continue to take the game to Partizani.

It was a cup final – anything could happen.

It had been seven years since Dinamo had taken the *Kupa* into their trophy room and the club had a good record in the competition.

The second half was the stage for our talismanic Sulejman Demollari to step up and write his name across the final.

Just like Eduard Abazi, he scored early and within four minutes of the restart to put us 2-1 ahead.

There was the predictable onslaught from Partizani, but we held out and, in the 90th minute, Sulejman sealed the deal with a second goal to have us run out as 3-1 winners.

I was 20 and had just won the first medal of my professional football career.

It's so important that you grasp these moments, take them in, savour them and remember what it was like.

From the near devastation of the previous season, the fight to stay in the top division, we had come back to roar into third place in the league as well as secure Dinamo Tirana's first *Kupa* since 1982.

The celebrations were fantastic and, of course, a first for me as a player. I suddenly realised how beautiful the game could be for everyone.

The look, on the faces of the Dinamo Tirana fans. The respite from the constant vigilance and oppression – the chance to celebrate a momentary victory. That was it – that is what you learn – live in the moment!

It was 1989 in Albania. There were no nightclubs, discotheques, bars. You had to fashion your own celebration.

When I look back at the moments of success that I have enjoyed with other clubs in different countries then that first win with Dinamo seems so innocent – and it was!

There was no alcohol involved. We celebrated in a natural way. There was plenty of water, coffee, fruit and veg available to us all, but the real elixir was seeing the joy on the faces of everyone around us.

Dinamo had another trophy in the story of the club, and our supporters celebrated the fact.

We now had a platform to launch for more success and that led to one of the best seasons of my career.

***

The season of 1989/90 was a pivotal one in my career.

In the first place, I had been elevated to the under-21 Albanian national squad and, in addition, I was made captain of the team, which was a huge honour for me.

It was my third campaign with Dinamo, and I could see the changes in me, not just as a footballer, but as a person.

I was, of course, physically in the best shape of my young life, working hard on my body, but just as important, I was mentally in a good place.

The standards were being raised around me and I felt I was a match for the task.

Dinamo Tirana were more than a football club to me. The Blue Submarine were a family. As I mentioned earlier, the way I looked at it, I had been somewhat of an orphan from the age of 14.

At that stage of my life, I had left Shkoder, my family and everything that I felt was important to me, so that I could develop as a person, as a professional player.

I have already said that it was forbidden to dream of a better future in Albania in those times. Forbidden to think that you could be better than you were, better in your outlook and disposition.

Communism was about control, and not just control of the body but also your day-to-day existence with the strictures on wages, housing, social interaction and so on. It was about control of the mindset.

The word 'brainwashing' once again springs to mind.

Yet here I was, an orphan, in a sense, a refugee from my hometown, in the capital of our country, trying to take my life forward.

FK Dinamo Tirana was becoming as important a factor in my life as the university itself.

Now I was learning from the finest education you could get – real life – and for that, there is no substitute.

The club were all-encompassing. They didn't just offer me personal and professional development. They offered me a bed for the night, regular sustenance from meals, a protective roof over my head and the comfort that I was wanted, valued, needed.

I had no objection to living at the stadium.

Why would I?

There were a few of us out there.

On the day before a game, we would be joined by the rest of the first-team squad who lived close at hand.

The idea was simple in its thinking.

You were encouraged, no, *ordered*, to think about the game all the time.

The next game was the big thing.

Do not lose focus about that upcoming 90 minutes.

I loved it. I never thought for a minute about what else I could or should do *but* live at the club.

In the first instance, I could not afford to live independently on the wages that I was earning. Was that deliberate from the club? Yes, possibly, but at that stage of my life, I was not too concerned about it. I had everything that I needed. Bed, board and a television when I wanted to watch it.

The season of 1989/90 justified everything about my ongoing development.

As a team, we tried to move on from the third place of the season before and improve on that – it had to be the first goal.

I do believe that, sometimes in football, you find a season when everything pieces together perfectly and, for me, in that campaign, it all did.

As a mark of our progress as a club, we were down to play in the first *Superkupa e Shqiperise.*

If you were looking for an equivalent in British football, this would be the Charity Shield or, in European terms, the European Super Cup.

It was the meeting between the winners of the *Kategoria Superiore* and the *Kupa e Shqiperise.*

Whereas the English authorities use the match as a Wembley showpiece to raise the curtain on a new season in July/August, in Albania, the final took place in the January of the following season.

I suppose, in a way, this was more a meeting of past form than current form. January of the next season could see two teams who held the upper hand in the previous campaign having very diverse seasons in comparison to the former.

That was potentially the case in January 1990 when we faced off against 17 Nentori on the 11th of the month in the national stadium.

We, as a team, were in top form and, in a repeat of the *Kupa* from the season before, our heroes on the day were Eduard Abazi with another fourth-minute goal and then Sulejman Demollari with a penalty close to full time that secured the first ever Albanian Super Cup.

My manager had deployed me in a completely different role for this game.

I was to operate as a number 6 – more of a defensive midfielder.

Instead of just defending in the backline, I was to work further forward, breaking up attacks, but just as importantly, to initiate and build our attacks from a midfield position.

I loved adapting to this position and must have got to grips with it as I ran out as the Man of the Match for the final.

I felt that we were completely dominant in the game and, personally, as a possible contributory factor in my performance, felt that I was helping to win the duels in midfield.

In short, we were worthy winners of the trophy.

It could be a pivotal moment in our season, but Bejkush Birce was adamant in his assessment.

Enjoy the moment, but do not get too overjoyed. Keep your feet on the ground and work hard for the ultimate reward in a potentially brilliant season.

It was not a problem.

My own assessment of success was that it made you hungry for more. You had tasted it and you wanted to taste that sweetness again, repeatedly.

We were now learning not just *hard* work, but *smart* work.

I, along with my team-mates, was learning to have a new mentality. Grow into your position. Your value to the team.

If one of the key players was not having his best game, help him out. Work for each other. Share the experience out on the pitch.

I felt that I was becoming a better version of myself – a more efficient football player who now read the game in front of him. Rather that reacting to situations, I was being more proactive and trying to look a few moves ahead.

It was paying dividends for all of us as we headed to play Partizani Tirana on the final day of the season, looking to secure the title for the first time in five years.

There was work going on at our ground, so the match was moved to the national stadium which probably added to the tension of the occasion.

The arithmetic was very simple.

We were three points ahead in the title race. However, the way the system worked out in Albanian football was different from anywhere else.

In most football federations, the onus would be not to lose the match and retain the three-point advantage over your rivals.

That was not the way in Albania and, perhaps, made for more excitement, albeit of the controversial kind.

If we drew – we won the title.

If we won – we won the title.

If we lost – we could still win the title, as long as we did not lose by three goals.

The rules would have handed three points and a superior goal difference to Partizani and they would have taken the title.

It was a tense situation, especially since we lost 2-0.

Sulejman Demollari uncharacteristically missed a penalty kick and, to be honest, we were, ultimately, holding out for the victory.

I have to say, in the final analysis, I felt we were lucky to secure the win, but a title is a title and the celebrations for that first league flag of my career were enjoyable.

Interestingly, I thought the celebrations for the Albanian Cup the year before were more intense and heartfelt.

Perhaps it's the slog to a title that drains the resources more or there is a sudden outpouring of celebration for a national cup competition with a one-off final and showpiece occasion.

Anyway, we had a chance to do the double that year as we were back in the final of the Albanian Cup with Flamurtari as the opponents.

We went into this one as league champions and the opportunity to do the double of league and cup for the first time in 30 years.

What a powerful incentive that was.

As champions, we were automatically installed as favourites for the cup, but a final is just that, 90 minutes to raise your game as you inevitably will and see where it takes you.

Flamurtari pushed us hard, and a 1-1 draw took us to penalty kicks.

In all honesty, that was not my strong point so I did not take one, but the boys made the difference in a 4-2 victory and so the cup was ours. What a season!

The Super Cup in January, league champions by the end of May and double winners in June.

To that date, the finest campaign of my life.

The transition in Dinamo Tirana in three years was extraordinary, as was the development of Rudi Vata.

As we celebrated along with our supporters, I felt ready to progress to the next stage and see where my football could take me.

## CHAPTER 7

# THE COST OF FREEDOM

Students of politics will always be able to identify the time and place when the forces of communism were blown away in Europe by political unrest and a deep-seated desire for democracy.

The Berlin Wall coming down was one such moment, but for me, personally, the fall of Nicolae Ceausescu in Romania around Christmas 1989 was the moment when I actually started to believe that change, *real* change, was coming.

Ceausescu had ruled the country as Enver Hoxha had done in Albania. Whilst forcing restrictions and hardships upon his very own people, and supported by a cadre of corrupt officials, he and his wife Elena had lived a pampered life in the communist state, but all that came to a bloody end in December 1989.

After fleeing their palace that month, Romanian television broadcast pictures of the couple apparently being tried and executed on Christmas Day.

The Romanian revolution appeared to be the bloodiest one as countries such as Czechoslovakia, Yugoslavia and in particular Poland were moving towards a seemingly peaceful transition to democracy.

Albania, right to the bitter end, remained the last outpost, the final bastion of post-war communism, but even that was changing.

I was 21 years of age in 1990 and remember full well the outcry from students in the capital, Tirana, for change.

Invoking the spirit of others in the Eastern Bloc countries, they mobilised and bravely marched on government buildings. I was a part of this revolutionary movement.

By that point, I was not only a professional club football player, but I had also made my full international debut for my country against Iceland.

However, equally, I was still a student and so, as my fellow collegiates marched, I joined them as well.

I cannot possibly claim anything more than that. There were so many who risked everything for freedom, but having grown up under dictatorship and oppression, I was certainly at one with my people. As I stood with them, side by side, and witnessed their heroic stance against the past, I started to resolve in my mind that my future would be taking me away from the land of my birth.

In football terms, perhaps unsurprisingly, at Dinamo, we were not scaling the heights of the previous season, but all things considered, that was beginning to feel of less consequence to me as an individual.

My uncle passed away on 31 December 1990 and Aleks and I were at the funeral on the first day of January. I little knew then that I would not see my brother for about five months. I am fairly sure that, at that point, he had not made the decision to leave Albania and take his chances in the West, but events moved so rapidly in the following months.

And so, we come to that moment in March of 1991 when my brother and some friends headed for the port of Durres, some 100 kilometres away from Shkoder, looking to jump on to a boat, *any* boat, and sail towards the West.

There were literally thousands of Albanians who were now doing this. So many, in fact, that the soldiers who were being told to stop, detain, even raise their weapons to those who were heading for freedom realised that they could not fight against the sheer mass of people.

People like Aleks were going up to them and identifying these soldiers as brothers, urging them to lay down their arms and join the people – stand *with* the people and *for* the people.

I cannot imagine the bravery on both sides that it took to do that and wonder about the basic humanity of people.

The revolution had started and Aleks was very much a part of it, although I did not know that at the time.

When word reached me that he had left, I immediately went to Shkoder to see my parents. Naturally, they were exceptionally worried for my brother as rumour accumulated upon rumour about those who had chosen to leave.

Boats that were ill-equipped to carry the thousands who wanted to flee were being utilised to do so and there were stories of them capsizing into the depths of the Adriatic.

I could not answer my parents' questions on the whereabouts of their eldest son, but I tried to assuage their fears.

Inevitably, my father asked me if I would be the next to go and I could not give an honest answer. The truth was that I was now sensing that this *was* my time to go. My time to try and escape.

Unlike Aleks, I had no necessity to run to the coast and attempt to jump on a boat. I was being given the opportunity to escape from communism by football.

It was the game that was giving me this chance.

The game that I had grown up with and loved.

All those hours of kicking a ball, in the soil, in my bare feet. Playing one-twos off the walls of my house and that of our neighbours. Practising, practising and practising even when I did not realise it.

The game had saved myself and my parents in the summer of 1987 when Herkuran Isai had signed that letter to confirm that neither I nor my father were traitors, and now the game was giving me the opportunity to break free and taste that freedom.

The match against France in March 1991 was only my second international appearance, but the timing of it and the location seemed fated for me.

France.

A country that believed in liberty, fraternity, equality.

A free country with that word 'equality' in its constitution.

This now could be my base.

In the opening chapter of this book, I outlined how I had engineered my move after the match and how that had led me to a refugee camp in Nantes.

My story from then on becomes what I have always talked about – the fact that I may have lived two lives.

There was everything up until March 1991 when I was an Albanian who lived under oppression and dictatorship and then there was this other life afterwards when I had fled to France. A life that I continue to lead, never forgetting the past and never taking my freedom for granted.

In the camp, I became aware of goings-on in my hometown of Shkoder.

On 2 April 1991, there was a student march for peace. It was a march that brought more than just students to it, but that day, four young men would pay the ultimate price for freedom.

As the gathering took place outside the Europa Hotel (which still stands to this day) and yards away from the main communist headquarters of the town, indiscriminate shots rang out.

A last act of defiance from an ailing regime on its knees?

A random, senseless explosion of anger from one individual against defenceless people?

Who can say?

All we know is that once the shooting had stopped, four students lay dead in the street as the march dispersed in wholesale panic.

It has become known as the 'last massacre of communism'.

For the record, I am proud to say, I list these martyrs here. For that is what they are. Martyrs.

Martyrs for freedom.
Martyrs for their beliefs.
Martyrs for peace.
Martyrs for their people.
Martyrs for their country.

A memorial stands today where they were felled by a cowardly, anonymous assassin:

*Arben Broci – 21.*
*Bujar Bishanaku – 22.*
*Nazmi Kryeziu – 22.*
*Besnik Ceka – 21.*

Dozens were injured that day, but these boys gave their lives for freedom. And one of them, Arben, was a friend of my brother, Aleks.

Had my brother and I not been in exile, he in Italy and me in France, it is almost certain that the two of us would have been on that protest march that day, potentially standing with these young men outside the Europa Hotel.

Standing together with all of the other students, demanding change. Who knows what our fates can be?

I found out in 2023 that there was another significant person in my life who was also demonstrating that day against the communist regime – my father.

This I learned from a chance encounter with Astrit Hafizi, my first manager at Vllaznia Shkoder and who, at the time of my defection, was assistant coach to the national side.

He had been in France along with me in 1991 but had returned to Albania. On 2 April he was out on the streets in Shkoder when he met my father.

In that winter of ’23, he recollected to me that my father appeared to be quite sad but had asked after me and Astrit was able to tell him that I had remained in France seeking asylum.

And then Astrit revealed to me that he had asked my father about the last words I had said to him before I left to play for Albania.

All my father could do was shake his head sadly, before placing it on Astrit’s shoulder and sobbing quietly.

This I had not known for over 30 years and the revelation left me in a state of high emotion, especially since my father had passed away shortly before in the summer of 2023.

When you are a young man, hungry for the world, desperate for freedom and in a rush to move forward, you sometimes do not take time to reflect on such matters.

It is only now, in these latter years that I have come to fully appreciate the suffering and the agonies my parents would have gone through in the aftermath of the defections of Aleks and me.

My father, although approaching 60 at the time, would still have been working, as was my 48-year-old mother. He had moved on from banking into the construction industry whilst my mother was a factory worker who analysed the flour for bread before it was processed.

At a time when Albania was going through the pangs of turbulence, uncertainty and insecurity, Aleks and I were not there to help ease that workload.

We weren't there to look out for them and so, although my memories of the period are about *my* fight, I cannot help but reflect on the anguish this brought to my parents – and yet, I had hoped they would understand.

My father had given us Italian, a second language, at dreadful risk to himself. I cannot believe that he did not see my future as being one outside of Albania.

Once I knew that Aleks was free and safe, I knew that I had to make the commitment to escape.

Of course, I worried about my parents. To lose two sons in such a short space of time and in such dangerous terms was something that they would struggle to bear, but I hoped, in my heart, that they would see why Aleks and I had acted as we did.

That note that I had made in my letter about hoping to have them join me in the future was not a half-hearted plea.

I was in earnest and once I had got a grip on my life and new-found freedom, I would be sending for them.

In April 1991, that was for the future as here I was now, in a refugee camp in western France. The authorities actually bought Adrian Zukaj and me the tickets to travel to Nantes and the camp.

Effectively, it was like a prison, albeit a prison that you could leave whenever you wanted.

In the three weeks that I was there, I would wander into Nantes, at my leisure, and marvel at the freedom afforded to the French people.

Here they could come and go as they pleased. Never having to justify their existence and yet, I felt isolated. I had not earned my place to be among these people and so I would go to the director of the camp and ask him if he would make an introduction for me to the local team, FC Nantes.

I had hoped to establish myself with a club, especially Nantes, but I had a meeting with their chairman which I felt was unproductive.

Indeed, to be honest, I found him to be rude, arrogant and intolerable as an individual. He looked upon me, I felt, as an Albanian refugee who was beneath him, his club and his country.

All I was asking for was an opportunity, but he treated me with utter contempt and so I bided my time in the hope that some other club would express an interest.

I had been a professional player for four years, an internationalist for my country and in the prime of fitness and health. I backed myself to go to *any* club.

There was another Albanian footballer in the country at that time, Josif Gjergji.

Josif, although a few years older than me, had been a team-mate at Dinamo and also played in the France match for Albania as I had, in the Parc des Princes.

He had also defected and, that night, in Paris, he had arranged to be driven away from the French capital to start a new life. I was supposed to be taken as well, but there was only one space left in the car and I was reluctant to leave Adrian Sukaj on his own, so I made a decision.

I said to Josif that he should travel to Nantes with his fellow Albanians and then send the car back for me and Adrian.

Josif set off that night with four of his countrymen and a driver who was Algerian.

At one o'clock in the morning, they had an accident in Le Mans.

Thankfully there were no fatalities although the car was a write-off and Josif sustained broken ribs.

Sadly, Josif would die suddenly and tragically, suffering a heart attack on the pitch whilst playing football in 1996 and to this man I owed the next part of my story in France.

Actually, I was privileged to play in a charity match to raise funds so that we could send his body back to Albania for interment after his tragic death.

The story of refugees in a car crash was local news, of course, especially as it involved an international footballer who had played against France.

The press, naturally, took an interest and visited Josif in hospital where he was able to tell them that I had also sought political asylum and was currently in the Nantes refugee camp.

Through this relationship, Josif, who was signing for French side Le Mans, was able to get a trial for me.

That was all I wanted.

A trial.

An opportunity to show what I could do.

Get me out on the pitch and see what I can offer. I knew that I would not let myself down because I was playing for my freedom. And so, I arrived at Le Mans, eager to show what I could do. Eager to justify some faith in me and have the club offer me a contract.

This would be another step on Rudi Vata's road towards freedom.

Le Mans had a defender, Joel Bossis. He was the brother of Maxime Bossis, the famous French defender who represented his country in World Cup finals tournaments.

At some point late on in the trial, Joel and I went into a tackle. It was the kind of thing you would see on any pitch, in any match on a global scale, but on this occasion, when I most needed to impress, I broke my ankle and tore my ligaments.

Perhaps my body was tired. Perhaps I was too eager to impress, but in that moment, when Joel and I came together in a crude challenge, I heard the *CRACK* of my ankle and watched as my foot filled with blood and my boot split open.

My world was upside down.

I had felt comfortable in the trial. The game had gone well for me, and I had given an honest account of myself in the hope that I would be offered employment.

Josif had been watching from the sidelines and he told me later that the coaches were impressed with me and my ability to marshal their defence for the future. All was looking good.

Yet, here was another trial. Another test.

My future lay in my ability to play football.

My value lay in that ability. I was not looking for charity. I was looking to establish myself as a professional footballer in a new environment.

And yet, in one trial match, I had jeopardised that possibility.

This was serious.

Not only was my career in jeopardy. I had sustained a bad injury as a footballer without a club.

I was not insured for the treatment or the recovery.

I had to accept this as another challenge, but I needed help.

Thankfully, that came in the guise of another individual to whom I am always indebted.

His name is Jean Rene Belliard and he was one of the club sponsors at Le Mans. This generous man undertook my medical expenses with a private doctor as, perhaps, like Hekuran Isai, he saw something of value in me as a player or as a person.

It was a wonderful gesture as I had no real means of supporting myself. Jean Rene told me to concentrate on getting better and then he would help me to find a club – and he did.

In the interim period, however, I tried to come back too quickly from the break and, in a pre-season friendly for Le Mans against Arsene Wenger's Monaco side, who boasted the talents of African Footballer of the Year, George Weah, I damaged the ankle once again.

Jean Rene's doctor was unequivocal with me. He knew that I had been lying to myself that the ankle was properly healed, and he told me that, had I continued to train and play then, in less than two weeks, gangrene would have set in, and my leg would have had to be amputated.

It was a sobering assessment and one I had to listen to as my career would have been completely over.

All I had ever known was football and I had to place that above any other consideration. That would be my way out of my predicament.

Jean Rene urged me to rest the ankle in a plaster cast and, at the proper time based on medical advice, return to training. He now had a club for me to go to so that I could get my fitness back.

FC Tours were an amateur team who played in the lower leagues of France and Jean told me to sign for them as a non-professional.

The club put me up in a fifth-floor apartment and, once my ankle was passed fit for purpose, I started my training again in earnest.

Part of that saw me rising at 5am every morning and going for a 10 kilometre run. Naturally, what with the injury, lack of training and proper football, my fitness levels were low, but I applied myself with my customary dedication to the task.

So much so that, within a short space of time, I got to a stage where I would vault the steps of my apartment building four at a time on my return. This I would do ten times in a row and, as you can imagine with the noise and the heavy breathing, my new French neighbours were, initially, not amused, but they got used to it!

By this point, remarkably under the circumstances, Aleks and I had been reunited and, once again, it shows you the fates of life.

When my brother had fled on the first boat that he and his friends could climb on to at the port of Durres, they had absolutely no idea where they were going or where they would land.

As it turned out, the boat berthed at Bari on the south-east coast of Italy and that is where my brother took his first steps as a free man in a free land.

As I have related, I found out that he was safe and well in Italy, just before I made my decision to seek asylum in France.

Through that network of friendship, Aleks was also to learn that I was in Le Mans and that is where he wanted to be as well.

But how to do so?

We were located in two different cities, in two different countries that were close to 1,900 kilometres apart and, crucially, Aleks had no passport.

And this was when fate was to lend a hand.

SSC Bari were, at that time, a Serie A club with a fantastic new home in the Stadio San Nicola. The stadium had been purpose-built for the Italian World Cup tournament of 1990 and, as a consequence, was a fitting arena for any major European final.

In 1991, it was to be the venue for the final of the biggest trophy of them all, the European Cup.

That year's final was between Red Star Belgrade of the former Yugoslavia and Olympique Marseille of France.

You want to talk about fate?

What were the odds that my brother would wash up onshore in the very city where the final was to take place?

Then again, what were the odds on one of the contesting finalists being French?

These were the two main driving forces that would, ultimately, re-unite the Vata brothers.

Aleks had a plan that was brilliant in its simplicity, yet risky – extremely risky.

He would leave the refugee camp he was in, somehow get himself an Olympique Marseille scarf and pass himself off as a French football supporter of the club. In this guise he could mingle with the crowds and hopefully travel up to France after the final.

Red Star went on to win the cup that year after a penalty shoot-out, but of more immediate concern for Aleks was to envelop himself with the thousands of Marseille supporters as they headed back home.

And there actually were thousands of them.

It was the era of Bernard Tapie – the French billionaire and charismatic president of the club. The era of players of the quality of Jean-Pierre Papin, English international Chris Waddle, Basile Boli, Manuel Amoros and Brazilian defender Carlos Mozer.

The era when this powerful team would win four Ligue 1 titles in a row.

An exciting team who were enthralling to watch. In a couple of years, the club would suffer the indignity of relegation as punishment for a bribery scandal, but in May of 1991, they were the best team in France and, as such, pure box office.

Was it any wonder that they took so many supporters down to Bari for the European Cup Final? And now, my brother would be among them looking to escape to France.

I knew that he was coming as friends had arranged for me to speak to him on the telephone in his refugee camp.

I would wait for him in Le Mans.

To understand Aleks' journey is to truly understand the cost of freedom.

I can't even tell you the route, but he travelled the whole way by train, having to hide away in the toilets whenever they reached a stop in case any authorities boarded looking for passports and any other form of identification.

He told me later that, for some ten hours, he hid himself away in the loft of a railway carriage, lying flat on his back and almost succumbing to suffocation.

Can you imagine the strength of mind, the willpower and the sheer desire to be free that inspires someone to put themselves through that kind of experience for that length of time?

Astonishingly, he crossed the border and made it into France. Unfortunately, there had been a certain amount of miscommunication between us that led to confusion.

I told Aleks I was in Le Mans, but possibly as a keen basketball aficionado, he confused that with *Limoges*, a city famous for their professional basketball club, CSP.

In other words, when he arrived in Limoges, he thought his journey was over only to find that he had to travel another 300 kilometres.

Clearly, someone at the station had sympathy with him and a phone call was set up with my friends in Le Mans who told him to jump on another train.

Having come so far, Aleks was not to be denied our reunion.

And so it was that after five months of no contact, a hazardous trip across sea and land, moving to a country with a different culture, lifestyle and language, it was a wildly emotional moment when Aleks stepped off that train and we were reunited on the platform.

The brothers Vata were together again and now we had a life to plan.

I was trying to recover from my ankle break, get myself fit and back to playing football whilst, thanks to my friend Jean Rene, Aleks was given a job as a welder at a local firm.

We were on our way.

*My parents, Pjeter & Sonya Vata.*

*Aleks and myself with our parents*

*On a day out with our parents.*

*Again, with our parents although we are a bit older now.*

*Enver Hoxha – the brutal, oppressive dictator who closed Albania off to the world for 45 years.*

*Me, aged six. By now, Holland's Ruud Krol was my first football hero.*

*Back row, second from right – Nearly 14 at the Loro Borici Stadium, playing for my school team, Xheladin Fishta*

*Representing Albania Under-21s at 18. The dream was always to play for my country. Dinamo Tirana – national champions, 1989/90. (back row; 2nd from right)*

*Aleks and I having dinner with our parents.*

*Aleks and myself with our maternal grandmother, Jelena. She had to make the biggest decision of her life in 1946.*

*Parc des Princes, Paris. From here, on 30 March 1991, I took my first steps towards freedom*

*My parents, Aleks and myself with Bernard and Martina Lory in France. A great couple who looked after me when I broke my ankle.*

*1992 – Coming to Paradise. I sign for Celtic the same day as Andy Payton (L) and Stuart Slater (R). My fashion sense kept my new team-mates amused.*

*A head shot. My own personal rebellion against the Albanian authorities was to have long hair!*

*The 1995 Scottish Cup Final against Airdrieonians. I was determined to have that medal.*

## CHAPTER 8

# PARADISE

Ultimately, and somewhat ironically, I was never awarded political asylum in France. The authorities came to this conclusion by deciding that I had not been persecuted in Albania for my political beliefs and, even that, as a professional footballer, I was presumably treated quite well by the authorities.

And so I remained a refugee and, in some ways, I still see myself that way. The status of my political asylum, or lack thereof, however, became a moot point in the early summer of 1992.

As described in the opening chapters of this book, I was approached by Bejkush Birce, manager of the Albanian national side, and was asked if I would consider, once again, playing for my country.

It was not a request I had anticipated. To be honest, given that I had left Albania and settled in France, choosing to eschew the life that I had been raised to live under the communists, I remember thinking that I would never represent my country out on the pitch again. It was something that I was willing to accept at the time, but here we were, a year on from my defection.

A year in which Albania had been attempting to develop not as an isolated state governed by dictatorship, but as a free, democratic country.

On the 31March 1991, the morning that saw me in a French Gendarmerie, asking for asylum, my country held an election.

Given the infancy of the freedom movements, student demonstrations and the overall chaos, the communists were, remarkably, returned to power.

This wasn't as ridiculous as it seemed when you factored in that, although there were many screaming for change, there would always remain those who maintained that level of fear that to oppose the communists was to result in outright punishment.

When a nation and a people have lived under the strangulation of tyranny for over 40 years, it is difficult to cast aside that tyranny in one fell swoop.

There is, I believe, a theoretical condition called *Stockholm Syndrome*, that argues a case for a hostage or a captive forming a psychological bond with their captor no matter how hostile or abusive their relationship can be.

It is an irrational condition, but it appears it can be an accepted way of thinking.

Perhaps that was the collective case with my country's people at that time. I personally think, impossible though it may be to prove, that the older generation of Albanians were so conditioned by the communist authorities that they found it hard to break the ties at the first time of asking.

This would be a slowly evolving project; the birth pangs were difficult, but within a year there was another election.

The communist juggernaut was slowing down and collapsing from the pressure of the people who now demanded change that the old order would not and could not provide.

In March 1992, a democratic government was formed in Albania for the first time since before the Second World War.

The Albania of the 21st century was being grown from these small shoots of freedom and I watched on with keen interest.

Could this really be the start of something lasting and peaceful within my country?

I sincerely hoped that it was, and hope is a powerful drug. Take that hope away from people and you can plunge them into chaos and despair.

Nothing could be taken for granted when it came to Albania, but I thought I could sense something new in the air.

And so I was delighted to be asked back into the international scene, especially with the World Cup qualifiers coming up.

Albania had been drawn in a very tough group alongside Spain, Denmark – who were about to become surprise European Championship winners in the summer of 1992 – Northern Ireland, Republic of Ireland, Lithuania and Latvia.

Our first match was in the Estadio Benito Villamarin, Seville on the 22 April against the Spanish.

Naturally, my team-mates were curious to see me, as was Bejkush Birce. He knew that I had broken my ankle in France, and that I had fought back from that injury enough to warrant a place in his squad, but he seemed more interested in how I had adapted to life outside of Albania.

It had been a year since I had seen him, but he looked well and was pleased that I had made the necessary changes in my life.

And yet, his question remained: was I fit enough for this challenge? I felt I was, of course, but there is physical fitness and match fitness – two quite different disciplines.

Out of that game in Parc des Princes, the year before, only three us were with the squad for Seville.

Josif Gjergi, of course, was in France as was Adrian Sukaj, my companion on the night I asked for asylum in that Gendarmerie.

Others had left the country for Romania, Belgium and Greece and had not returned to the national squad.

It was, therefore, an untested group of players who formed my team-mates for the game against Spain.

It was such a feeling again to walk out on to a pitch as an Albanian internationalist. I was representing my country, once more.

A new country.

A more optimistic country.

Arguably, I hadn't played a meaningful game of football for quite some time, what with my period in French lower leagues, serious injury and rehabilitation, and now I was to face one of the best countries in the world.

And yet, one works hard for these moments. It is a test.

God-given, you could say. How hard was I willing to work? How much could I take?

I had to take that positive energy into the game.

No negativity, Rudi.

Stand up for yourself – for your country.

Was I really a different person?

How had freedom shaped me?

Had I maintained my discipline and my fight?

Ninety minutes on a football field could, perhaps, answer those questions for me.

We lost 3-0 to a good Spanish side, full of world-class players, but I felt I had performed well against the experienced and dangerous Real Madrid striker Emilio Butragueno.

*El Buitre* (The Vulture), as he was known, had scored four times in a 9-0 rout of my countrymen about 18 months earlier, so to subdue him on this particular night was a sign that, despite my injury in France and a year out at this level, I was still equipped to do a job.

I was pleased with my contribution.

I hoped to carry it forward into our next match which would be a game and a day of huge personal and professional consequence for me. Although, naturally, I could never have guessed that at the time.

The day that my life would mark another turning point came on the 26 May at Lansdowne Road, Dublin, when I walked out on to the pitch to play against the Republic of Ireland.

I have already written that I played a very good game and caught the eye of none other than the Celtic manager, Liam Brady.

As to the match itself?

Given that we were up against potentially the best Irish national team in their history, which had been quarter-finalists in the 1990 World Cup, I felt we put up a strong showing.

They knew they were in a game.

We managed to frustrate both the Republic and their supporters for an hour before conceding a John Aldridge goal and, even at that, it was still close to 80 minutes when Paul McGrath scored a second to take the points.

It was certainly no disgrace at all.

It was in preparation for our next fixture against Lithuania that events took a turn for the unexpected.

I was receiving a massage from one of our national team physiotherapists when he casually asked me if there was any news on my Celtic situation.

On *what*?

I was stunned and had to ask him to what he was referring.

According to his inside information, after the match in the Republic of Ireland, Liam Brady had been speaking to officials from the Albanian Football Federation. He was overheard to say that I had had a good game and that I was the type of player who could do a job for both him and Celtic. How could he facilitate a move?

The forces of communism may have fallen but the old tendencies to secrecy were still in abundance, so no one from the AFF informed me of Liam's interest! In fact, in my opinion, they deliberately withheld this information from me.

For what reason?

I suspect pure and simple jealousy.

There was clearly still some loyalty to the previous forces that refused to sanction success abroad for an Albanian professional footballer and this wasn't just any football club – it was the famous Celtic of Glasgow.

I had the chance to become the first Albanian player to play for a major British club – and they did not want me to know about it.

Jealousy – what a toxic emotion!

I had been made aware of interest from a Greek club, but this was Celtic.

My mind was a cyclone. What an opportunity, and yet had it passed me by because of the petty politics and hypocrisy of the individuals in my national football association?

What was I to do?

Where was I to go with this information?

Who could I talk to and, more importantly, who could I trust?

Certainly no one connected with the Albanian Football Federation.

There was only one man, my honest and reliable Jean Rene Belliard and so, when I returned to France, I asked for his help.

To Jean Rene, an educated businessman of the world, the answer was simple enough. He would just phone Celtic and ask on my behalf – and he did!

As the fates would have it, there was a secretary at the club who could speak French and, between this lady and my friend an agreement was reached for me to speak to Liam Brady – in Italian, as you know!

On such twists and turns can one's life pirouette.

Celtic Football Club.

The name, the reputation, the traditions of one of the biggest names in world football and yet ...

I was settled in France. I enjoyed the country, the culture, the people and the climate and felt very comfortable there.

However, the chance to develop at a new club and not just any club, was the attraction to leave and go to Scotland.

Plus, I had used the word 'comfortable' there.

Rudi Vata was not at ease with 'comfort' in those days.

He wanted the challenge.

He *needed* that challenge.

I think there was a compensation payment to Dinamo Tirana for around £50,000 and I do believe that my good friend, Jean Rene Belliard, made some money out of the transfer, but I had no issue with that, to be honest.

He had become a father figure to me in that year in France and helped me when some others would not, in what was the most difficult period of my life.

It is my belief that he offered that help with no advantage for himself, so if he was helping me to go to Celtic then I was happy for him to take some profit from the deal.

God had guided Jean Rene to me.

I travelled to Paris with him to secure my British visa which he, incidentally, helped me with as well as paying for my flight to Scotland.

And then, I flew to Glasgow.

As usual, there was the discrimination to undergo when I arrived at passport control in both France and Scotland.

This was something that, although humiliating and patronising, was commonplace for me and any of my people who could travel abroad.

I always felt that we were looked down upon as Albanian nationals and, over the years, I have tried to stand up to this treatment as well as encourage others to do so.

Even now, with the transit across borders of so many Albanians, there is a perception that we are not necessarily to be trusted and this plays to a particular narrative for people of a certain political persuasion.

It was still that way back in the summer of 1992.

However, once I had retrieved my luggage, I was met by a club official who transported me out to Celtic Park.

I was not the only player signing for the club that day as I discovered when I arrived at the ground.

I was introduced to Liam Brady, and he explained to me, in Italian of course, that I would be travelling with the club out to Ireland for a couple of pre-season friendlies.

In addition, I was joined by a midfielder called Stuart Slater and a centre-forward, Andy Payton. The boys were both English so I wasn't the only one who would be acclimatising to a whole new environment. They, naturally, had one up on me as an advantage – they, at least, spoke the language!

There is a picture of the three of us, new recruits, standing together, holding up the obligatory Celtic scarf for the press and photographers.

I do remember some of my new team-mates at the club making fun of my dress sense which, they felt, was rooted somewhere around the mid-1970s!

That day, I was wearing white socks with white trainers, and I had to accept that I was behind the times and quite ignorant of what they called *style*.

My hair was long at that time, and this was a deliberate rebellion for me against the straitjacket of communism.

You can imagine that, in a country like Albania where the growing of beards was forbidden, then long hair was something liable to get you into a great deal of trouble.

The Beatles with their invigorating music and all-encompassing, global influence were certainly never, ever heard on Albanian State Radio.

As a child, I remember the tiny radio that my mother had and how, on a Sunday evening, she would position it discreetly in the kitchen to a point where she could pick up transmissions from across the border in Yugoslavia.

Yes, this was another communist country under the rule of Josip Broz Tito, but opinions varied on him from being an authoritarian despot to one as a more benevolent dictator.

I will leave that to the historians to argue over, but I do know that, on the crackly airwaves of my mother's transistor, I was able to hear music that was not just Albanian folk.

I even got to hear the King of Rock 'n' Roll and the ultimate example of the decadence of the West to our Politburo, Elvis Presley – and I have always liked him!

One of the first things I did when I defected to France was to allow my hair to grow as long as I pleased. This, to me, was another little victory in my fight for freedom. My Ruud Krol moment, if you like.

So, what was it to me if my new team-mates took the mickey out of my look – at least I was choosing to *have* that look!

I tell you something now – I did not know that Liam Brady was Irish. Can you believe that?

I had grown up with Italian football and followed his career.

I knew that he had won Serie A titles with Juventus,and had also played with Sampdoria, Internazionale and Ascoli.

I knew how he played, what his style was but I had never known his nationality.

Never even thought about it.

I tell you; I could feel the history at Celtic Park, and it motivated me to leave a mark at the club, however small that might prove to be.

I was proud that I was the first Albanian footballer to play in the United Kingdom and felt that I was representing my country.

The people at Celtic made me feel very welcome and this epitomised their ethos as a family club.

Everyone from the doorman through to receptionists right up to coaching staff and management cared for me in a special way.

I think they could tell that I needed that care as I was a stranger in a foreign land and, if I was to take this huge step forward, then I would need as much help as I could get.

In that respect, they were all very patient with me.

As I outlined earlier in this book, Liam identified that I would need to get up to the pace of the game in Scotland as quickly as possible. And so, after training in the morning and eating lunch, I was to report to Rab Douglas for those punishing 100m and 200m sprints.

Never had I worked so hard on a training ground and never had my body felt the way it did after those rigorous workouts with Rab.

As I testified, I would lie on my bed in the city's Albany Hotel with my body literally shaking from the exertions.

This was the Celtic way – Liam's way – of getting me fit for the contests ahead and I was determined that I would not let him or, for that matter, my country down.

Everywhere now there were new experiences for me to address and, fundamentally, one of them was a real challenge.

I needed to learn English and with the extra work that I was putting in, it would have been impossible for me to go to college and study the language, so I devised my own method.

The Rudi method.

It sounds ridiculous now, but whenever I could, I would sit down in my hotel, television on, an English–Albanian dictionary beside me and watch every single soap opera that I could get on the screen! *Brookside*, *EastEnders*, *Coronation Street*, all of the Australian ones such as *Neighbours* and *Home and Away*, these became my teachers and I, their pupil.

I would sit and write down phrases, read my notes and learn the structure of the words as well as their pronunciation.

It was a slow, onerous task, very time-consuming, but I felt successful for me and, gradually, the pieces of the jigsaw started to come together.

Having said that, however much English I was learning from watching actors on television, it bore absolutely no resemblance to the *English* that I was hearing from some of my team-mates in the Celtic Park dressing room!

Charlie Nicholas!

Peter Grant!

Joe Miller!

Great guys all – but I had absolutely no idea what they were saying to us and each other! They would pelt things back and across at each other all the time, in those loud voices, fall about laughing together and I would just sit there trying to understand it all.

That is the common currency of dressing rooms all over the world, of course. In Scotland, I learned the word *banter* and came to appreciate it – what it was and when it got used.

They did, however, make me very much a part of it all.

Peter Grant was a man steeped in Celtic and its history and a man for whom, it seemed to me, playing for the club was never a job – it was a mission. I got the feeling he would have done it for nothing, just to be a Celtic player.

He was a top professional constantly reminding us of the demands of the club and its supporters.

Work for the club.

Put the effort in.

The demands were everywhere.

You needed the will to fight – fight for yourself, fight for the club, fight for the support. I knew that I had joined a special club.

However, it was my belief then and remains so to this day, that, if you are a top professional, you do not need to be told how to do the job.

You know what it takes to make that grade.

The discipline.

The courage.

Live the proper lifestyle. Look after yourself and the rewards will come to you and not just with baubles and trophies but with the feeling that you are doing the best you can and not cheating yourself, the support or your team-mates.

There was genuine football quality as well in the Celtic Park dressing room.

In Paul McStay and John Collins, I felt there was talent that could play for any club in the world.

John, of course, would go on to do so with AS Monaco where he won the Ligue 1 title as well as playing in the UEFA Champions League before a later career with Everton and Fulham.

Paul certainly had the ability to do that and, to be honest, could well have earned more than what he was on at Celtic, but he remained, loyally, a one-club man.

A quiet-spoken guy, but what a player and he was my captain as well.

The man I looked up to out on the pitch as well as on the Barrowfield training ground and the dressing room.

The Celtic I understood was all about their history and, of course, I knew that a great deal of that history was wrapped up in the great rivalry with Glasgow Rangers.

I had played in the Tirana derbies for Dinamo against Partizani, but I knew Celtic–Rangers was a global fixture in the context of world football.

One of the glamour games in our sport.

Celtic v Rangers had resonance all over the planet.

My arrival at Celtic came at a time when the club were struggling against the power of Rangers, but it was still a mystery to me, when we had players of the calibre of Paul and John for example, that the team were struggling to keep pace with their city counterparts. Liam Brady was new to the management game and would need time to develop his plan for the club.

I formed a good relationship with both Andy and Stuart, which was natural as we were the latest additions in the dressing room and developed quite a bond.

Andy and I were both staying in the Albany Hotel and he was a real asset to me as I came to understand the culture and customs of this strange city that I was living in.

Yes, there is no question that the first few months were difficult in terms of acclimatisation and getting my fitness up to par, but my view had always been to embrace the challenges and make sure that I come out of the other side as a far more developed individual.

Andy, and to a certain extent Stuart, helped me in that development.

I worked hard in training and was becoming a regular in the reserve side under the guidance of Frank Connor.

Frank was an old-school coach in his methods, but I respected him hugely, especially as a big part of his remit was to build you up mentally as well as physically.

He would constantly be talking to you, telling you that you were getting closer to the first team and that you had the talent to do a job when you got your chance.

That chance came to me at the start of October.

Celtic had started the season indifferently, I think it would be fair to say. There was a brilliant night at home in the UEFA

Cup when I sat in the stands and watched the boys recover from a 2-0 first-leg defeat to FC Cologne of Germany by winning 3-0, but domestically, all was not so well.

The team had been knocked out of the Scottish League Cup by Aberdeen and were behind in the title race as well.

A disappointing 2-1 home defeat to Partick Thistle was adding to the pressure on Liam as manager.

There seemed to be an issue out on the right wing, and he had tried various ways to combat that problem.

Stuart Slater was more of a midfielder, as was Brian O'Neil. Joe Miller preferred to play up front and through the middle, but all three had been tried on the wing.

On the day of the Thistle game, I was with the reserves against the same opposition and had scored in a 2-1 win. In actual fact, I had been scoring quite a few for the second string eleven.

Liam Brady decided to start me on the right wing for a game away to Dundee.

It was the 3 October 1992, and I walked out on to the pitch at Dens Park as a first-team player for Celtic Football Club.

There wasn't a huge crowd, but as I was soon to realise was normal, the away support seemed to outnumber the home. Such was the pull of Celtic.

Mike Galloway put us in front after just three minutes, but we never added to that lead and managed to stay ahead to claim the points with a 1-0 victory.

I came off with about 20 minutes to go with Stephen Fulton coming on as substitute, and felt happy with my contribution.

The right wing was a totally new position for me, but if that was where my manager wanted me to play, then I would have no argument with him.

By that point, all those 100m and 200m sprints I had been doing with Rab were paying off. In addition, I felt *as* fit, if not more so, than others in the squad.

Running had become my thing. I had always looked after my body throughout the days at Vllaznia and Dinamo and, even in the year I had in France, my recovery from the ankle break was based upon constant exercise and workouts.

Rab and the rest of the coaches at the club had now taken my fitness to new heights and I was more than prepared to rampage down the right flank or do the many overlaps that Liam would insist upon.

I think, overall, my manager was also pleased with my debut, but when I came off, he dressed me down a bit for my decision-making at one point.

There was a moment in the match in the second half when my endless running had seen me get into a one-on-one position with Dundee goalkeeper Paul Mathers.

I had come through the middle and had to make a decision. Should I try to finish it off or should I perhaps square the ball to either Andy Payton or Stuart Slater?

In the event, the heat of the moment perhaps, I tried for goal and cracked the ball beyond Mathers only to see it rebound off the post.

It was a close thing and would have been the ideal way to cap my debut off with my first Celtic goal, but Liam told me that, if a team-mate was ever in a better position to score, then I should pass to him and see if he could finish off the move.

I respected Liam, listened to him and nodded my head.

That first goal for my club would have to wait, but as it turned out, not too long.

Aberdeen were always hard opponents in my time at Celtic and, having already knocked my team-mates out of the League Cup, as I mentioned earlier, they arrived confidently in Glasgow on the first Wednesday night in December for a Premier Division fixture.

I started on the bench that evening and watched on as my friend Stuart Slater ended a 20-game goalless sequence by putting us ahead in the first half.

Stuart's joy and relief was there for all to see and I, of course, was glad for him.

He was my friend as well as my team-mate and I knew he had been feeling the pressure at not finding the back of the net.

However, Aberdeen hit back to be 2-1 up at the break when my manager told me that I was going on along with Andy Payton.

The moment that I had been waiting for since I had come to Glasgow arrived early in the second half when Andy worked something inside the box, poked the ball forward among a ruck of red shirts and I was there to shoot past Dons' goalkeeper Theo Snelders.

What a feeling!

There were an estimated 30,000 supporters inside the ground that night and I will never forget the roar from the crowd or the looks of delight on the faces of the Celtic fans whom I could see as I galloped towards the Main Stand to celebrate.

The goal would never have been described as a classic, but I had worked hard to get into the position and taken my chance.

As it turned out, that was the last of the goals although, if I remember rightly, we had the better of the chances and perhaps should have won the game, which seemed to sum up Celtic at that time.

For me, football is all about the fans and, even now, with the changes in the fixtures that seem to be dictated by the big television money, competitions and stadia that I see, the game will always be a working-class sport.

I feel that it's the working-class supporters who made the real noise at Celtic Park. That night, I heard, for the first time, my name being chanted to by those same supporters.

Yes, I had run to the Main Stand as that was the direction of my momentum, but I came to understand that, in those days, the most noise, the most fervour came from that holiest of places at Celtic Park – The Jungle.

Here was a congregation of my kind of people.

The stand was great, of course, and certainly more comfortable from a viewing perspective, but I felt that area was the preserve of what you might call the *professional* classes: lawyers, architects, accountants – the people who, conceivably, ran the country. But it was in The Jungle that I could sense *my* people.

And, I felt, they could sense me.

I was a working-class Albanian, who came from a background of hardship, in the material sense.

Everything that I wanted to achieve could only be done so by the old-fashioned qualities of hard work and determination.

I would not be found wanting in either department.

I felt The Jungle knew this and, when they would start that slow rhythmic chant of *RU-DI! RU-DI! RU-DI!* – I felt they were identifying with me and my roots.

Their passion for the game and the players was a deep-seated thing and I suspected that they were representing generations of working-class people who had come along to *Paradise*, as they called Celtic Park, for decades.

A tradition of handing down a love for one's club with dignity and respect for the players.

Yes, *my* kind of people and there was always that special energy that I would get when I heard my name ringing out around the ground.

Of course, I was far from the only one – there were quite a few in our ranks that received and merited the same treatment – but I liked the fact that my first name of only two syllables lent itself so well to a chant.

One such honest, firmly grounded person of good working-class stock was a fellow by the name of Joe Martin.

Joe lived with his family out at Glasgow Cross, and he was in the Albany one day when I was having lunch.

As a big Celtic supporter, he had no problem recognising me and so he approached my table.

He just wanted to say hello, but we immediately made a connection, even though, at that time, my English was embryonic.

We are still pals today and that was founded upon the friendship he offered to me back in my earliest times at Celtic.

Joe it was who would give me a lift out to Celtic Park for training and matches from the hotel. I did not have a driving licence back then as I had never driven a car before although I had a small motorbike during my time in France.

Joe it was who invited me to meet his family or just go out for dinner. My lack of English and Joe's novel approach to improvisation would see us sitting at a table when he would imitate the noise of a cow to indicate steak on the menu.

The grunting was for pork, of course, but the funniest of his techniques was when he would set out his arms like a couple of wings and pretend to be a chicken.

What we must have looked like out in the restaurants of Glasgow I can only wonder about!

He was also instrumental in one of my greatest memories of my time at Celtic and it came the weekend after the Aberdeen game.

We had taken our revenge over Partick Thistle with a 3-2 win on Saturday when Joe showed up the day after at the Albany to see if I wanted to go out.

I naturally said yes, but when he told me we were going to a bar, I did have second thoughts.

I didn't drink.

There was a night when the Celtic boys took me out to a club and tried to get me to down a few vodkas with orange, but it really wasn't my thing.

However, Joe told me I wouldn't need to drink as it was more a social thing.

To this day, I cannot remember what bar he took me to, but I remember one thing, it was a Celtic bar because all across the walls there were items of memorabilia festooned in green and white with the history of the club laid out in front of me.

Another thing I noticed was that it was jam-packed with people.

Good, working-class people, like Joe, out for a grand time and to celebrate all things Celtic.

No introduction was required from Joe for them to see who I was – these would have been some of the supporters who cheered my equaliser against Aberdeen a few nights before and they wasted no time in showing their appreciation.

I was raised, bodily, up in the air by the crowd and carried to the front of the bar. The whole time they were shouting, singing, congratulating me and, of course, taking the opportunity to chant my name just as they would in The Jungle.

It was a whole new experience for me.

One that I enjoyed even if I was a bit bewildered, but it felt good to be among these honest people and to realise that my actions out on the park had given them a moment of total joy.

To be able to see that, experience it, was a very humbling moment for me and, as I say, one that I have never forgotten.

And I owe that to Joe Martin – one of the kindest men, with the biggest of hearts, that I have ever known.

A true working-class Glaswegian who took the time to form a friendship with a foreigner who could barely speak his language.

Life is often about perspective and moments like that one in a Celtic bar in the east end of Glasgow provide you with an opportunity to reflect upon your good fortune.

Here I was now, in a good place, earning my living at a great club and, above all, doing it as a free man.

## CHAPTER 9

# TURBULENCE

I *was* in a good place and probably more relaxed and happier than I had ever been allowed to be before in my life.

I would wake up in the morning and could barely wait to get out to the ground and get on with team training.

If things were great in a personal sense, they were arguably less so on the professional front in terms of the direction of the club.

As I mentioned about my first season, Celtic were eliminated from the League Cup. We narrowly lost games against Hearts and Dundee United 1-0 consecutively over the Christmas period and by the same score in a New Year defeat at Ibrox to Rangers, meaning our resolve to win the Premier Division was being sorely tested. Even in that loss, a game that I missed, the boys had the bulk of the chances but home goalkeeper Andy Goram was in fine form, as he always seemed to be against us, and our league challenge was dissipating in front of our eyes.

I had learned that Celtic had a fine tradition of cup football, particularly the Scottish Cup. This was a competition that, even to this day, they have won more times than any other club in the land.

That year, the team had struggled to get beyond lower-league Clyde and needed a replay to do so, courtesy of a solitary goal from our striker, Tommy Coyne.

I was restored to a struggling side by the time we headed through to Falkirk to play in the next round of the cup.

Unlike Clyde, the Bairns, as they were known, were in the Scottish Premier Division but they were having a hard season that would lead to relegation and, in addition, they had never beaten Celtic in a Scottish Cup tie.

We lost 2-0, which meant our domestic campaign was effectively over … and it was only the first week of February.

I was shocked by the defeat so I can only imagine how Liam Brady felt about it all. Incredibly, no one had explained to me that the game in Falkirk was a straight knockout. I had assumed that this was only the first leg of the tie and that we could win through at Celtic Park.

Liam was under immense pressure now, although I was perhaps a bit naive about it as I felt he would remain in charge of this project for a few years regardless of any setbacks.

But, the history of Celtic Football Club was built not just upon success and silverware, but also a mix of quality, attacking football and going to the end of the season with a challenge for all the available trophies.

Everybody was unhappy with the way things were going out on the pitch, but equally, behind the scenes there was great unrest.

Of all the times to be at this great club, that period in the early 1990s was arguably the most turbulent of all.

The bridge between the supporters and the men who ran the club was completely broken. As they say, there was 'something in the air'.

This was to manifest itself towards the end of my first season and gain even more momentum in my second. When we were out on the park, the supporters never retracted their backing for the team and the players, and we were grateful for that.

It was always a sight to behold to be playing in front of such a great crowd and feeling that love for the team. I know that word 'love' can be misconstrued but I defy anyone to tell me that it is not the best word to sum up the rapport between the Celtic support and their club.

Even though the times were hard, there was still that passion and even optimism on a matchday that something magical could happen.

I enjoyed my rapport with the supporters. As I said, I think they identified with me as one of their own. A worker – a player who gave everything to the cause – a working-class kid who knew all about struggle and was willing to pay any price to succeed.

There were small, special, personal moments in my first season when, in the cauldron of a big game and us winning a throw-in right in front of The Jungle, I would pick up the ball only to hear someone call out my name.

At the utterance of *RU-DI!* I would turn around and wink my eye at whoever it was. I revelled in those moments – that personal contact between myself and a supporter.

Due to the implementation of all-seated stadia in Britain after the Hillsborough disaster in 1989 when 96 people lost their lives at an FA Cup tie between Nottingham Forest and Liverpool, The Jungle stopped being a standing-only area at the start of my second season at the club.

The area was still somewhere that afforded a great view of the game, but I have to say, despite understanding the safety requirements at the time, I felt that the power of The Jungle was diluted by that decision.

And I don't think I was the only one.

I missed the swaying masses and the endless sea of faces that greeted us when we took to the pitch.

In time, the whole stand would be knocked away and replaced as part of the new Celtic Park for the 21st century.

Sometimes, just like my relationship with Joe Martin, you could strike up a friendship with a Celtic fan.

Ricky Fearon was another example of that, and he also introduced himself to me at the Albany.

He was a different animal to Joe as he was a bit more extrovert, I would say.

Always dressed in the best of stuff, flashing a wee bit of jewellery around but a down-to-earth guy in the best traditions of the Glaswegian. He undertook to upgrade my dress sense and image one day by gifting me a brand-new velvet jacket.

Yes, it was flash, but I felt good in it, and I thanked Ricky for it. My status in life was changing and I was a modern professional footballer.

Inevitably, there came a time for me to leave the Albany, as living in a hotel is not really the healthiest way to structure your life.

The club advised me to look at renting a flat and so, along with Joe Martin, I went along to see a few places.

Eventually, I settled in Hamilton, just outside Glasgow and, indeed, live there to this day although in a house with my family.

In those early days, as a bachelor, I found a flat at a place called the Furlongs which, as you can imagine, was close to Hamilton Racecourse.

Having a flat gave me a grounding, somewhere to return to at the end of the day so that I could continue looking after myself properly as well as work on my increasing grasp of the English language.

At the Albany, I had relied on taxis or the kindness of Joe Martin to get me out to Celtic Park for training and matches, but that again was a situation that had to change.

John Collins it was who saw my transport dilemma and took it upon himself to do something about it.

Celtic had a sponsorship deal with a local car dealer, so John, who stayed quite close to me, took me down one day to look at a few cars.

He insisted upon it, and I don't think he really believed me when I said I did not have a licence to drive!

Remember, my upbringing in Albania had prohibited my family from using the car that they owned and, as I have already explained, the automobile would just sit in our garden for, literally, decades, unused and rotting away.

In France, there was the small motorbike that I used to get around but that clearly was not sufficient for the commute from Hamilton into Glasgow.

To be honest, I am not sure Liam Brady would have been happy with the notion that one of his players was risking their body on the main arteries into Glasgow on the back of a moped!

John insisted on helping me and, with that help, he selected a car which I took for a test drive.

I say 'drive', but I doubt John had ever experienced anything like it then or even now!

I had a rudimentary idea of how it all worked, what with clutches, gears, brakes and steering, but just like my English, it was one thing to read about and have the knowledge – it was quite another to apply it to practical use.

And so, John and I jolted along, stuttering our way down the road like a couple of clowns at the circus!

As I revved the engine, shredded the gears and accelerated at the wrong times, John howled with laughter.

I had to admit, it was hilarious for me as well, but as you may know by now, I stick to my tasks and work to develop my skills.

When the test drive was over and we both alighted from the vehicle with our bones shaking, I knew it was another area of my life that I would have to work upon!

Those were the light-hearted moments I look back upon. The camaraderie of team-mates helping each other out, the laughs that we could share that helped to bond us as a unit. But still there remained the problems behind the veil at Celtic Park.

The notion of directors, shareholders with stakes in an institution, was a new concept to me. It had never been that way in Albania.

Certainly, Dinamo Tirana had vested interests but my experience there was that the club was run by that one man – the Minister of the Interior, Hekuran Isai, head of the mistrusted and fearful *Sigurimi*.

As illustrated previously, he ran the club as his own personal and political fiefdom and was a man who, as you know, with the stroke of a pen and a signature on a document, had the power to deliver me as a first-team player or place me and my family in exile.

I often hear now about individuals holding all the power in a club. An oligarch, for example, whose word is law and must be obeyed. These men have become increasingly involved in English

Premier League clubs, for sure, but I wonder if they have more power than Hekuran had back in those days?

It's one thing to interfere in a club's day-to-day affairs regarding players; quite another to have the authority to destroy a player and his family by expelling them to hell on earth.

I did not know, when I arrived in Glasgow, that Celtic, at that time, had many financial problems and that they were mounting.

To be honest, I would not have considered it any of my business. I was there to play football and represent the club out on the pitch, but you could not hide the headlines and rumours that were going around.

As I have mentioned, I feel Paul McStay could have made a lot more money than he was on in Glasgow and, naturally, we would hear rumours about the wage bill across the city at Ibrox, but for my part, having come from a poor background, I was just happy to be earning a decent salary.

My ambition had always been to play at a top club and let's be fair, you only really get one chance to come to Celtic.

I had taken that chance. Made the decision to leave a country, a culture and a climate that I enjoyed, to see if I could develop both as a footballer and an individual.

I was enjoying my time in Glasgow, but I was not so daft that I could not feel the tensions around the ground or, indeed, sense the pressure that was on Liam Brady, especially as we started the 1993/94 season.

It has been said that coming second in Glasgow was not acceptable and the Rangers juggernaut at that time was hard to stop.

I had dropped out of favour with my manager and, with the situation being that a team could field 11 players with room on the bench for only three substitutes including a goalkeeper, then it was clear that my matchday involvement was limited.

The season brought the same old inconsistencies with the team drawing their first three league fixtures against Motherwell, Hibernian and Rangers, which meant we were playing catch-up as early as the end of August.

Liam brought me back into the side for a home match against Aberdeen in early September, but the 1-0 defeat was to be my last start under the man who had brought me to the club.

The stuttering league campaign continued and with my team heading up to Perth to play St Johnstone in October having taken only nine points from a possible 18 and been knocked out of the League Cup by Rangers at the semi-final stage, it was clear that Liam was walking a tightrope to remain in control as manager.

The end came when St Johnstone won 2-1 on that Wednesday night and Liam tendered his resignation, having mulled it over throughout the bus journey back to Glasgow.

What else could he do?

He had been the first Celtic manager never to have played for the club and now he became the first Celtic manager to step away of his own volition.

Liam Brady was a big enough man with vast experience in the game and he knew that his position was becoming increasingly untenable, so he did the honourable thing.

Me? I was heartbroken.

Yes, I was disappointed that I did not get more game time under my manager, but I understood that he was the man making the decisions and I would just have to work hard and try to impress on him my value to the team.

That was football at all levels of the game, but Liam was not devoid of the personal touch either.

I cannot forget that first Christmas I had in Glasgow.

As you know, that was not a thing in Albania and even in France it did not seem to be celebrated with the fervour that it received in Scotland.

I remember walking through the lights in George Square, Glasgow that year, a little bemused as to why it was such a big deal, but Liam Brady, with his knowledge of the world and realising that this was my first experience of the festive season in Scotland, invited me to his home on Christmas Day to share a meal with his family.

That, to me, was the mark of the man.

He cared for me in a way that I imagined he cared for all his players. Yet, maybe in me, he saw something a bit different.

Yes, we had both left our own countries to earn a living abroad, but he understood that, in my case, I had also escaped to pursue my freedom.

I think Liam was big on character and the way a person conducted himself. In time, he would try to take me down to Brighton when he was manager there and that told me enough about his regard for me as a person as well as a player.

Liam Brady had brought me to Glasgow and allowed me to realise a personal and professional ambition by coming to a big club – and now he was gone.

As I say, I was heartbroken.

And yet, I had to remain practical as I had a living to earn and a new manager to impress.

In Lou Macari, Celtic now had someone who seemed to fit their established club model.

Unlike Liam, he had played for Celtic and, also unlike Liam, he had managerial experience, having worked at clubs such as Swindon Town, West Ham United and Stoke City.

I knew nothing about him and, I have to say, for the first few weeks he was in the job, I felt that he ignored me.

His attitude appeared to be a very cold one, but over a short space of time, I completely changed my opinion of the man.

He brought me back into the first team and we started to have a different kind of chemistry.

It was always going to be difficult to regain momentum in our season given the start we had had in the early stages of the campaign under Liam.

Lou Macari did not have it easy.

The spirit in the group was not at its best at this point and became potentially worse when we were knocked out of the Scottish Cup in late January, by Motherwell.

A great deal of that unrest was placed at the feet of the board of directors as the gap between them and the support grew wider. There was a real fear factor around the club. People, frankly, were worried about their jobs as rumour after rumour took hold and the media reacted to it.

Stories were being bandied about concerning the lack of money, investment or working capital at Celtic Park.

It wasn't difficult to view the mood of the camp when one could see these looks on the faces of the people around the club going about their daily business.

I could argue that the players' wages were better at some of the Ligue 2 clubs in France and I was quite surprised at how low the salaries were, comparatively speaking, at such a big institution as Celtic.

By now I was an established international player who had already captained my country at under-21 level and the changes in my life were very apparent. Now I was Rudi, the professional footballer. Rudi, the homeowner. Rudi, the car driver.

These were things that I did not think I would have been able to say had I stayed in the Albania that I had left behind.

I wanted to develop further. I was stronger and fitter than I had ever been at any point in my life, and it felt good.

I loved being at Celtic, but if the club did not want me or was going bust then I would have to be prepared to move on.

It seems hard to credit now but there was a justifiable fear at the time that Celtic would cease to be and, indeed, if a man called Fergus McCann had not come into the picture that may well have been the outcome.

Everyone is familiar now with the Scots-Canadian businessman and entrepreneur who saved Celtic Football Club.

At the time though, he appeared to be a complete mystery to us all and certainly seemed to be to the media as well.

To my knowledge, he only ever appeared in the dressing room once in my time at the club and it was so insignificant that I can't even recall why he was there.

I got the impression that the football side of things was certainly not his area of expertise, so he avoided it to concentrate on what his plans were for the club.

You only have to look at the stadium and the success that Celtic have had since those intensely nervous days in the 1990s to see that he followed through on his plan.

Lou Macari seemed to chop and change the team a lot.

Initially, I had a run of games under him and then I was back out again only to reclaim my spot in the spring of 1994.

Despite everything that was going on at the club, I was enjoying my football, and this culminated in a goal against Hearts at Celtic Park. It came just before half-time and gave us a 2-0 lead with John Collins having already netted.

It was perhaps indicative of the malaise around the ground though that our opponents pulled a goal back in the second period and then an equaliser in the last few minutes of the game. That seemed to sum up our season.

It was great to be back in the team although, the following weekend, at Rugby Park, Kilmarnock, my campaign came to an end in the most horrible of circumstances.

Just one minute into the game, I went up for a high ball with Kilmarnock defender Andy Millen and as I did so, I seemed to fall over his shoulder and landed face down on the pitch.

My left arm was under me, and the pain was excruciating as it shot up through my limb.

It was, of course, a complete accident, of the sort that can happen and does happen on any number of football pitches around the world, but as I tried to push off with my left hand on the ground, I realised it could not take the pressure.

The arm was broken in two places, and I started to panic about it.

The physiotherapist came on to the turf and the pain was so bad that I was given morphine.

My season was over and, naturally, as a player you start to worry about the wider aspects here – could this affect my career?

There was an upcoming testimonial match against Manchester United at Old Trafford, but I was never going to make that showpiece occasion. I was also having contract talks with the club and was on the point of signing a two-year deal, even though I knew there was interest from Borussia Dortmund in Germany, but I soon found out that an injured player has no value when he is out of the game.

No training. No matchday. No involvement and I found what I perceived to be an indifference from the club.

In the fullness of time, they were to offer me another contract, but it was a reduced one from the original offered by Lou Macari.

I did not feel that was particularly honest.

I resigned myself to making a full recovery and getting ready for the new season. Over the summer, I would rehabilitate and be prepared for everything to kick off again.

It would be my third season at the club, and incredibly I was also about to move on to my third Celtic manager in that time.

## CHAPTER 10

# REDEMPTION

He looked me in the eye, and I respected that, but I did not like what I was hearing.

It was very clear.

It was very concise.

And it felt like a bomb going off around me.

*What I mentioned in the meeting a few minutes ago, was not meant for you. It was Liam who signed you and he wants you at Brighton.*

And then there was a pause, before he said, in that quiet, deliberate way that I would come to know well …

*I think you should go.*

*This* was my introduction to Tommy Burns.

* * *

We had all arrived back from the summer holidays and were preparing for the new season.

Lou Macari had been dismissed from the club although he would subsequently take Celtic to court to challenge the decision – and lose.

I didn't know much about Tommy other than the fact that he was viewed as a legend from his playing days at the club.

Ironically, he had been in the Kilmarnock dugout as their manager that day when I crashed to the ground at Rugby Park and broke my arm and I do recall that he showed genuine concern, which I respected.

I was still rehabilitating from the injury when we reported to a meeting with the new manager, but I knew that I would soon be back to full fitness and was looking forward to developing my Celtic career further.

As team talks and first impressions go, I was quite inspired that day.

Tommy promised us that we would all get a fair chance to make an impression on him. He had obviously seen some of us play but not too many close up and he would be making up his own mind about us.

That was perfectly reasonable.

He was committed to Celtic; committed to taking the club back to the success of previous years and the feeling I got was that he would be great for the team.

In addition, the support would immediately buy into him because of his previous status as a player and a Celt.

Arguably, at 37, he may have been viewed as a bit young an appointment for such a big club, but he had got Kilmarnock promoted in his first season at Rugby Park.

Given that they hadn't been in the big league for a decade, it certainly hinted at his potential.

Tommy seemed more expressive than Lou had been, to my mind, and certainly more passionate as well.

Only time would tell where he could take us, but I had already decided that I was looking forward to training and working under Tommy Burns.

As I said, I was very inspired.

So much so, in fact, that I decided to tell him that to his face so, a little later on in the day, I knocked on his door.

He invited me in, and I immediately expressed my view.

*I am very impressed with what you said in the meeting, gaffer. As you know, I am rehabilitating from my arm injury, but my recovery will be quick. I am a hard-working and dedicated professional who will prove to be an important member of the team.*

And that was the point when he spoke the words that opened this chapter about his speech not being meant for my ears and that I should go to Brighton.

I was profoundly shocked, and he would have been fully aware that I had signed a new contract, as he continued …

*You are not a part of my first team plans so, it's up to you. It's your future, but I am looking to bring in some new players.*

On the one hand, he was willing to respect the new contract, but he had clearly made his mind up about me and yet, hadn't seen what I could bring to his team.

The last he had seen of me was when I was lying on the turf at Rugby Park after the first minute of the match.

How could he possibly judge me on that?

My emotions were in turmoil.

Here was a man who I thought I could respect. A manager I was looking forward to working under; a manager who had, quite literally, assured everyone in the room that they would get a 'fair chance' and less than an hour later, had reneged on that promise to me. Unhappy and angry, I left his office to go and think about my future.

How could I respect a man who had apparently been so dishonest to me?

Here, now, was a dilemma for me.

I was at a club with a manager who did not want me there.

Another arc in my learning curve was about to begin.

I am an 'action' person. It is all very well to go into a Catholic chapel, light a candle and pray, but unless you can back up your prayers with action then I fail to see the point.

I knew what I had to do. I needed to convince Tommy Burns that I *was* a part of his plans and so, when I was given the all-clear to return to active training, I seized it.

However, Liam Brady did phone me and I did go down to Brighton for about a week. I felt at the time that I perhaps *owed* him something.

He wanted to get me into training and convince me that he had a club that wanted me.

It was flattering, of course, and heartening that the man who had brought me to Celtic felt that, in his words, I could 'do a job' for him.

The training was good, and I felt quite relaxed about the set-up.

Liam had me playing in different positions, in other areas of the pitch and I was getting into the box, scoring goals.

All the time, he would say to me, 'Come to Brighton. They don't want you up there. You can do a job for me down here and I will take care of you.'

I didn't doubt any of his rhetoric, especially the last bit.

Liam Brady had already proven to me that he could, indeed, take care of me as my first Christmas in Glasgow will testify.

It was tempting. I liked Liam. He wanted me. The money would be good … and, yet.

Celtic.

The lure of the club, the people within it, the support.

In Glasgow, I felt I could identify as one of them. I have written about this before. The working-class tradition, honest graft, dedication.

All of that I felt in that city.

Brighton, as a town, had its attractions, the climate being one of them, yet I did not think of myself as someone who belonged on the south coast of England.

Perhaps, just perhaps, it was a bit too comfortable, dare I say, middle-class?

I could have been wrong and everything like that is perception, but I always trusted my instinct … and my instinct was telling me to stay in Glasgow.

After a week of training, I looked Liam Brady straight in the eye, shook his hand and was honest with him.

*I appreciate, so much, what you have done for me and that you want me to come to work for you but …*

I paused, and then … *my heart is still in Glasgow.*

Being the man he was, Liam accepted my decision.

He knew I was not the type of person to short-change someone. When I gave my word, I gave my word.

I had come down as he had asked, worked hard in training and impressed enough for his offer, but in the final analysis, he would have known that I would always be true to my heart.

Possibly, in fact, *probably*, he thought I was making a big mistake, but he never said so and he had my respect for that stance.

And so, I returned to Glasgow and Celtic.

My determination, as ever, was to make Tommy Burns recant his opinion of me.

And that started back in the reserves under the gaze of Frank Connor.

I threw myself into the team, working deliberately hard in training and, all the while, trying to give the first team manager a decision to make.

Frank loved me.

And I do not believe that is too strong a word.

He *loved* me.

Once again, he was telling me to remain patient, to keep my head high, maintain my standards and wait for my opportunity.

The reserve team was successful. We had young boys in there like Simon Donnelly, Malky Mackay and Brian McLaughlin who would all go on to play for the first team as well as Stuart Gray, who sadly passed away at a young age while I was writing this book.

My engine was still good. I was back at full fitness, getting into the box and scoring goals.

The team were motoring well, and we were winning a trophy into the bargain – which was something that was eluding the first team.

This was the season when Celtic Park was under reconstruction, so the club decamped to the national stadium, Hampden Park.

That meant that when the boys reached the final of the League Cup, at the end of November, the match was played at Ibrox.

I was still out of favour with Tommy Burns, so I sat in the stand and watched us lose out to First Division side Raith Rovers, 6-5 on penalties after extra time.

It was a devastating result for the boys and the manager.

In particular, I felt for my captain, Paul McStay, who missed Celtic's final penalty, allowing Rovers to sink their kick and lift the cup.

There is a picture of Paul disconsolately walking off the pitch with Charlie Nicholas. He had a haunted look on his face and appears close to tears.

The club hadn't won a trophy in over five years and were expected to overcome a side from a lower division, even if they were at the top of their own league.

The search for some silverware continued and I kept my composure, head down, working on my football.

By March, the club were out of contention for the Premier League title, playing to gain a place in Europe for the following season and only the Scottish Cup remained as an option to win a trophy.

I was aware that Tommy had been monitoring my work throughout the season and I had no doubt that Frank Connor would have been posting regular reports to both him and assistant manager Billy Stark.

Billy it was who spoke to me the night before a midweek league match away to Kilmarnock.

'Tommy has seen you working in the gym and knows how determined you are. He wants to play you tomorrow. Are you ready?'

'Of course,' I said. 'I still believe I can play for Celtic.'

And that was it.

21 March 1995.

Almost a year since I had last played a first-team game for Celtic, ironically against Kilmarnock when Tommy Burns was their manager.

A year in which I had recovered from a double break in my arm.

A year in which, for the majority of the time, I assumed Tommy was ignoring my efforts to force my way back into his plans.

And a year in which I had developed more strength of character to deal with his rejection and that mental toughness meant that I *was* ready to play for Celtic again.

I was to play right-back that night with Tom Boyd vacating the position to form a centre-half pairing with Tony Mowbray.

It was a tense evening, partly because the boys had knocked Kilmarnock out of the Scottish Cup a couple of weeks before, but there was another issue.

There was an ongoing compensation claim by the Ayrshire club for Celtic taking Tommy to Glasgow the previous summer.

The dispute was bitter and acrimonious, but out on the park, you do not think of such things although the home support, as I recall, were making their feelings known, especially to our manager in the dugout area.

We won 1-0 thanks to a late Andy Walker diving header and I was pleased for the team as much as I was about my own performance.

Paul McStay and I were picked out by a sports journalist as having a good game.

Now that I was back in the team, I had something to play for – as did the boys.

The Scottish Cup would be our only chance to win a trophy and we were in the semi-final against Hibernian.

The match, which was to be played at Ibrox, was to be shown live on television, unusually on a Friday night.

As I mentioned, Tommy had brought me in as a right-back, but for this one, he moved me into midfield.

It was at Ibrox, of course, only six months before, that Celtic had lost that League Cup in a penalty shoot-out and our bad luck on that front continued when Andy Walker saw his spot kick saved by Jim Leighton in the Hibernian goal.

The match finished 0-0 and so it was back to Ibrox again the following Tuesday for the replay.

Tommy had moved earlier in the year to sign Dutch striker Pierre van Hooijdonk and he had been an instant success, but he pulled up in the first match and so was unavailable through injury for the second encounter.

We may have been unfortunate with the penalty miss and possibly a bit nervous as well, given what was at stake, but there was no sign of that in the replay.

We deservedly won 3-1 thanks to goals from John Collins, Willie Falconer and Phil O'Donnell.

The last one came at a good point, the 82nd minute when Hibs were really pushing for an equaliser, and it delighted me that Phil scored with a header from my free kick into the box.

That rounded off a great night and, once again, I was pleased with my performance in both matches.

I felt free.

I had earned my place back in the side and was playing with conviction. My confidence was extremely high – so much so that I was looking to take any set-piece opportunities and try my luck from distance.

Such a chance came my way at Hampden Park at the start of May when Rangers arrived for the final Glasgow derby of the season.

They were champions again and we were all fighting for a place in the Scottish Cup Final team so, as always, we thought it would be a hotly contested game.

It remains my favourite Celtic–Rangers match, which is hardly surprising given that we won 3-0.

I recall it as being one of those spring days when the weather was just right and, all around the ground, you could see supporters in shirt-sleeves, t-shirts and scarves. Also, out on the park that day was French internationalist defender, Basile Boli, who had joined Rangers the previous summer.

On seeing him, I briefly thought back to that evening in March 1991 when we faced each other, representing our respective countries, at the Parc des Princes. That was the night when I took my first steps towards true freedom. How long and, indeed, how short four years can be in life and yet, the changes were all around me.

Football had given me the means and the opportunity and here I was at the Scottish national stadium playing for my club in one of the biggest matches in the world – Celtic v Rangers. The press were calling it a 'dead rubber' but try telling *that* to both sets of supporters.

All our goals came in the second half and that started with Pierre, free from injury, back in the side and hitting a low drive past Billy Thomson in the opposition goal after a brilliant solo run from young Brian McLaughlin.

A lot of people who were there that day will possibly remember that Rangers' Australian defender Craig Moore turned a Simon Donnelly cross into his own net to double our lead, but may not recall the sublime, backline-splitting pass that Paul McStay delivered into Simon's path that led to the goal.

It was trademark from *The Maestro* and, as I said earlier, Paul could have played in *any* side.

And then came a moment, approximately nine minutes from full time when we were awarded a free kick about 25 yards from goal, close to the right-hand side of the box, after a handball infringement.

Pierre always liked a dead-ball situation to exploit but he had been substituted a few minutes before and was off the pitch.

John Collins also had a capacity for taking great free kicks and had scored from such a set piece before against Rangers, but as we both stood over the ball, I have to say, as they would in Glasgow, I fancied my chances.

John was standing to the right of me, and it is perhaps possible that everyone in the stadium and watching on television expected him to curl a left-footed shot towards goal. It's even possible that Billy Thomson, standing on his goal line, prepared for that eventuality.

All I can say for certain is that my confidence was high and, in trying the unexpected, I took a short run-up, struck the ball with my right foot and it curled behind the three-man wall that Rangers had constructed before creeping into the net, eluding Thomson's left hand.

Ah now – what a moment.

No Celtic player ever forgets a goal he scores against Rangers – ever!

And I was off!

Racing back towards the halfway line, arm outstretched and drinking in the roar from the Celtic support in the stadium.

My team-mates clambered around me, offering their congratulations.

With the score at 2-0 and playing out the last ten minutes plus stoppage time, a goal for Rangers would have made for a nervous ending to the game but now, at 3-0, the match was effectively over.

We had put a seal on the victory and a smile on the faces of every Celtic supporter around the world – and that's what football can do.

For me?

A great personal and professional moment.

One commentator, in his match report, would describe me as the *rejuvenated Rudi Vata who had been brought back into the team late in the season.*

That suggested that I had been energised by my return to first team action and there may well have been a case to be made for that, but I had always maintained that my energy levels never deserted me.

I had worked hard to be in this position and when the time came, I was ready to play for Celtic and ready to take that free kick against Rangers.

Looking back on it now, there could not have been many Glasgow derbies that saw the winning margin determined by a Dutchman, an Australian and an Albanian!

It was a good victory to set us all up for the path to the Scottish Cup Final at the end of the month.

## CHAPTER 11

# SIX YEARS

*I want you all to play like Rudi. He always gives me 100% out on the pitch and in training.*

I looked around the room as Tommy Burns made this announcement. We had top players in that dressing room as I have mentioned and now my manager was singling me out as an example to them all.

It felt good.

In that moment, I felt a coming of age.

Tommy had been monitoring my progress and taken the decision to put me into his team and I knew I hadn't let him down.

I had given him, in his own words, 100%.

The expression now is that you 'leave nothing out on the pitch'.

That wasn't just my attitude to football, it was also my attitude to life.

The Scottish Cup Final was upon us, and we were up against Airdrieonians who, just like Raith Rovers, were from a lower division.

Nothing could erase from the mind that League Cup Final back in November.

The pain and agony felt by Paul McStay after he missed the vital penalty that handed the trophy to Rovers – it was etched on his face.

As captain for four years, he was yet to lead his Celtic side to a trophy and Celtic captains have to be winners.

That's the backbone of the club.

To be completely honest and, I say this as one who was not involved with the squad for the League Cup Final, I did feel that Celtic had not necessarily approached that match with the right level of respect for the opposition.

It was a game that they simply had to win and had not done so.

Possibly, as I said, it may have been nerves; the strain of expectation weighing on the squad, but something did not feel right to me at the time.

And now, there was a chance to make up for that day and it lay waiting for us at Hampden Park.

Note that, even though we had played all our home matches at the ground that year, the cup competition belonged to the Scottish Football Association, and they wanted it played at the national stadium.

I sensed a distinctly different atmosphere in the build-up to this one.

It was very serious and, unquestionably, there was that fear factor hanging around the club. Although Tommy and Billy Stark did all that they could to take the pressure away from us, the players and to put it on to them, the management team.

Tommy Burns.

Peter Grant.

Paul McStay.

Packie Bonner.

All stalwarts at the club who had been involved with its successes over the years.

They, more than anybody, knew and felt the winning traditions of Celtic Football Club.

We *must* win trophies.

That weight of expectation is on you when you walk out on to the pitch wearing the colours, representing the support and the history.

As Tommy Burns himself put it so eloquently: *When you pull on that jersey, you're not just playing for a football club, you're playing for a people and a cause.*

27 May 1995 wasn't just a chance to pick up the club's 30th Scottish Cup for the people and the cause, it was an opportunity to halt the barren spell of six years without a trophy.

We felt we had enough to defeat Airdrie.

Our closing run-in to the end of the season had been a strong one, what with overcoming Hibernian in the semi-final and, of course, that 3-0 victory over Rangers.

We had to concentrate on keeping a clean sheet and scoring a goal, at least – minimum requirements.

The club had taken us to a spa hotel called Seamill Hydro as this was the established pattern and headquarters of Celtic squads throughout the years in preparation for a big match.

You could feel the tradition in this fine hotel, down on the Ayrshire coast.

Celtic sides had come here over the years to prepare for European nights, cup finals, Glasgow derbies and more.

Countless players who had brought distinction to the club had used this place as their base camp under such famous managers as

Jock Stein, Billy McNeill, David Hay and now, Tommy Burns. I felt certain that I would be in the team that would start on the day of the match.

I had been playing well in all the games I had been selected for and, as I pointed out earlier in his team talk, Tommy highlighted my 100% commitment to the cause.

Unlike for the Rangers match a few weeks previously, the weather was not the best.

The gala occasion of a major cup final would always be something that you would want played on a beautiful day with the sun streaming into the stadium and the crowd lapping up the sunshine as well as the festivities.

The day of the Airdrie cup final was not like that. It was grey and overcast but you don't look for a weather report before taking to the turf.

It wouldn't have mattered anyway.

There was a job to be done.

As we walked out on to the Hampden pitch that day I can recall one thing in my mind – I am going to have that medal.

I knew one thing for certain – I wasn't going to let anyone down with my performance.

My manager – my team-mates – the Celtic support gathered around us – they would not be able to question my commitment.

Perhaps the early grey skies played a part – perhaps that weight of expectation that I mentioned earlier played a part – or perhaps both teams were scared of losing, but the 1995 Scottish Cup Final will never be regarded as a classic.

It was settled by a goal as early as the ninth minute when Pierre leapt higher than anyone else in the box to head emphatically home from a brilliant Tosh McKinlay cross.

Pierre had been an injury doubt before the game and actually didn't make it to half-time as he had to be replaced, but his header was the difference on the day.

For my part, I was pleased with my overall performance. My role was solidity and, having set that target of a clean sheet, I think as a defensive unit with big Packie in goal, Tom Boyd and young Mark McNally in the centre and Tosh out on the left, we worked well to subdue anything that Airdrie could put to us.

As I say, not a classic, but when the final whistle goes, and you get to see Peter Grant actually crying out on the pitch, you know that something special is happening. He had been named, quite rightly, Man of the Match.

It was rich reward for his persistence and passion to get us across the line as winners.

Pierre was the first Dutchman to score in a Scottish Cup Final and I was now the first Albanian to lift a major European domestic trophy.

Tommy Burns appeared to me to be quite cool about it in the immediate aftermath of the game and certainly both he and Billy let us know that the performance had not been our best, but he knew what it meant and his embrace with his former team-mates Paul and Peter told you all you needed to know.

Sometimes, it's only the result that matters.

We had done what we set out to do – bring a trophy back to Paradise and the six-year wait was over.

I had the chance to reflect on the events of the past year.

In the first instance, when Tommy had told me that I was not a part of his plans, there was a natural anger on my part and, if I am honest, I can say that, in a sense, I hated him.

However, I had to accept his decision and bad energy is a destructive force that will always work against you.

Hating people is not and never will be a solution.

I had to step back and accept the way Tommy viewed things and then I had to channel my energies in other ways – but it was not easy.

Then again, what had ever come easy to me in my life?

I suspect it was never my way to be programmed for an easy life.

I remembered those long walks with my father as a child, down on the shores close to the Adriatic.

I recalled how he would talk about the storm coming and you having to withstand it until it subsided, as it surely must, and then getting on with what you have to do.

I had to withstand the storm of that eight-month period at Celtic when I was not within a breath of a first-team spot.

And, as I did so, I forgave Tommy Burns for his view and the dishonest way that I felt he treated me in the early days of his stewardship of the club.

It is true to me that the example of Jesus on the cross, offering forgiveness to the very people who are persecuting him in his torment and agony, is a powerful one.

How easy it is to hold on to rage and let that negative energy corrode you.

The harder thing was to forgive, focus on the positives and go forward. It is as true in life as it is in the world of sport.

As I emerged from that storm and found myself back in Tommy's plans, I grew to love the man.

He had been big enough to go back on what he had said about my not being in his plans in the previous summer to giving me a starting berth in a team that had now won Celtic's first trophy in six years.

All of this was in my mind as I walked around the pitch at Hampden with my team-mates passing the cup to each other and savouring the moment.

If you look back now at those post-match celebrations, you can see that someone has given me a large yellow Mexican sombrero to wear – and I do so, proudly!

That would have been typical of the Celtic support gathered there that day.

A trophy was won.

We were returning to a newly constructed Celtic Park.

And now they had hope – and hope is life.

To me – if you have no hope – you have no life.

There was hope for Celtic.

Hope for the support and there was now some hope for Rudi Vata.

CHAPTER 12

# THE CHANGING CURRENT

*You know, you're saving us a lot of money from having to buy a right-back, Rudi.*

It was Packie Bonner saying that, my team-mate, and a goalkeeper of rich magnitude. In that dressing room, my dressing room, Packie was the most experienced Celtic player.

He had been at the club since 1978, won titles and cups, played in some of the most historic matches in the modern story of Celtic and had seen it all.

At the end of the 1993/94 season, Lou Macari had chosen to release him along with other Celtic stalwarts such as Charlie Nicholas, but upon his appointment as manager, Tommy Burns had reinstated both players.

Subsequently when, a year later, Tommy had led the boys to a Scottish Cup with Packie back in goal, the manager's decision had seemed vindicated.

Equally, I understood perfectly well what Packie meant when he used the word *us* in that short exchange.

It was clear that he was more than just one of Tommy's first-team players. He had Tommy's ear, as the saying goes, and little wonder.

They had trained together, played together, socialised together and would have enjoyed an almost brother-like relationship. In time, they would form a managerial partnership at Reading Football Club in England, so the makings of that partnership were perhaps gilded in Tommy's first year as Celtic manager.

I knew when Packie spoke like this he was also echoing the thoughts of Tommy Burns.

Although, to be honest, I had heard my manager's compliments for myself a short time before in a testimonial match down in Liverpool at the start of August, for veteran Everton goalkeeper, Neville Southall.

Although it was technically a 'friendly', both sides were in the final preparations of their pre-season work and we had Newcastle United and Liverpool coming up to Scotland over the next two weeks.

It was a competitive outing for us, and Everton were running us a bit ragged in a first half when they went 2-0 ahead – and comfortably so.

Certainly, Tommy Burns thought so and laid into us all at half-time.

*The only one giving anything for us out there on the park is Rudi – no one else!*

He continued in this vein for some time, pointing out our weaknesses and the fact that we had to perform, even in a testimonial game.

The message sank in, and John Collins produced a world-class performance for the second 45 minutes, first with a penalty and then starting and ending a glorious move to draw us level with a pinpoint strike.

He was the focal point but everyone in green and white had upped their game in that second half for the 2-2 draw and I was happy that Tommy had noticed, and not for the first time, my commitment to the people and the cause.

That season of 1995/96 seemed to promise much.

Tommy was building a team that reflected his ethos of hard work and entertaining football. There was a trophy to be displayed and the club were back at their spiritual home of Celtic Park.

In addition, he had added more direct forward play with the acquisition of experienced German international striker Andreas Thom, who arrived with a reputation for quality.

For the opening two months, I was a first pick for the team, and we started reasonably well, certainly better than the year before.

I recall a match at Pittodrie against Aberdeen in September when we were 2-0 down early on but rallied to be 3-2 up at half-time, which went on to be the final result.

There was no doubting the work ethic in the side and the will to win but then came two matches against Rangers.

The first was a midweek League Cup quarter-final tie at Celtic Park under the lights when we dominated possession and shots but still lost 1-0. There was a moment close to the end of the game when I pushed a cutback into the box. Rangers' captain Richard Gough knocked it away but only into the path of Paul McStay, who cracked a beautiful shot that said *'Goal!'* only to see goalkeeper Andy Goram push it away with an outstanding save.

It seemed typical of our luck against that Rangers side at the time.

Being knocked out of the cup was bad enough but when a similar performance of our domination was not good enough in a 2-0 league defeat at home to our rivals, Tommy went into the transfer market to bolster his squad and secured Jackie McNamara from Dunfermline Athletic.

He went into the side at my expense on the day he arrived as the team went to Falkirk for a midweek league fixture.

Jackie could play right-back and right-midfield, so he obviously represented direct competition for me.

I had no issue with that. In fact, I relished the challenge. Naturally I did. That is football. There is always competition for places in the starting 11 and, of course, this is healthy for the survival of a club.

For my part, there would be no relaxing of my standards or fitness and Tommy Burns would have known and appreciated that fact.

I felt my performances had been consistently good and no one could ever question my attitude or commitment to the team.

However, I was not a fool. I knew that you don't go out and spend over £600,000 on a player and not put him straight into your team. Subsequently, I started a few games on the bench, coming off it in a home fixture against Aberdeen to replace Andy Walker with the team 2-0 up.

I was pushed down the right flank and felt I had acquitted myself well.

I understood, though, that I would have to take any chance that came my way to get back into that starting 11 and hoped that my versatility would be an asset.

Jackie's arrival in October meant that he was unavailable to play for the club in European competition and we had already gone through to the second round of the European Cup Winners' Cup.

We had been drawn against Paris Saint-Germain, which meant a return to the French capital for me and, of course, PSG played their home matches at the Parc des Princes.

I was going back to the scene of my most life-changing moment.

Nostalgia is a powerful sense, an almost physical presence and as our team bus wound its way around Paris en route to the stadium, I could feel the emotions of that night in 1991 coming back to me.

This was where my new life had started.

The reason I was sitting on this bus as part of the Celtic Football Club first-team squad was directly linked to the night, four years previously, when I picked up my sports bag, left the Hotel Concorde Montparnasse and sought my freedom in a Gendarmerie.

I reflected upon the strides I had made in that time.

The year in France.

The broken ankle and recovery.

The match against the Republic of Ireland.

Liam Brady and the phone call in Italian that took me to Glasgow.

I was a citizen of the West now. The things that I had dared to dream of back when I was a child, growing up in Albania, had come true. I was earning my living as a professional footballer and had the freedom of choice so long denied to my compatriots.

There was the nice house that I owned with the nice car parked outside of it. Good neighbours, team-mates, friends. The opportunity to come out of the house, go where I wanted to go, speak freely to anyone whom I chose to engage with.

All of the things that many people would take for granted, would never, ever be that for me.

I would always appreciate them, but not in an avaricious, materialistic way. No, it was more precious than that to me.

Choice. This was what I had now.

I had choice and, when you have choice, you have freedom as the starting point.

Football had given all this to me, and I was grateful.

It was in this period of reflection that I opened up a little to Packie, who was sitting beside me on the bus.

I don't think that, up until that point, I had ever fully explained my life path to a team-mate.

He, of course, had known what it was like to leave one's country at a young age to further one's career as he had left his native Ireland and come to Glasgow, but he had not had to make the sacrifices that I had.

I told him the whole story and how emotional it was for me to be back in Paris at the Parc des Princes.

He sat, listening intently and finally said, *Jeez, Rudi – you should write a book!*

Well, here we are, my friend!

Paris Saint-Germain were a really good side and, in fact, would go on to lift the trophy that season, but we put up a great showing on the night to narrowly lose 1-0.

Despite their pedigree, we were confident that we could turn the tie around back on our own soil.

In the early stages there was not much between the sides. However, from a long clearance by Paris goalkeeper, Bernard Lama, I challenged one of the French forwards in the air. I got my header away but landed awkwardly on the turf.

A pain shot right through my shoulder akin to a dislocation; however, I managed to get to my feet and continue with the game, but I was feeling it.

If you look back at footage of the match on YouTube, you can see me occasionally rubbing my shoulder and trying to rotate my arm. In the heat of the battle, you must put such things out of your mind and focus on the job.

We won a free kick about 30 yards from goal when future Celtic player Stephane Mahe went in heavily on Pierre van Hooijdonk only for the Frenchman to come off worse from the challenge and have to leave the field injured.

The ball was pushed to me from the set piece, and I swung a cross into the box from which Andy Walker got away a strong header, but Lama made a good save.

I had a reasonable partnership with Andy for that sort of thing and I was honoured when my name appeared in his personal choice of a Celtic Xl from the guys he had played with, years later, but on that occasion, Lama was equal to the task.

We had chances but fell behind to two goals from Patrice Loko before half-time and that was the tie effectively over.

As was my Celtic career.

The shoulder was beginning to stiffen, and I felt that I could be a liability to the boys so, when I came off at half-time, I had the physio check it over.

As I suspected, it was dislocated, and I was unable to continue, with an immediate visit to local hospital, Ross Hall, recommended.

Simon Donnelly was sent on in my place not, as was suggested by one of the newspapers, to pep up our attack. The move was not tactical, it was enforced by my injury.

I didn't know at the time that, as I made my way off the pitch and down the tunnel, I would be doing so for the last time as a Celtic player.

How could I know?

The boys lost 3-0 on the night, but as I said, Paris Saint-Germain went on to claim the trophy so there is no shame in being knocked out of a tournament by the eventual winners.

I now had to concentrate on my recovery.

A dislocated shoulder is difficult, but it is an injury than can heal very quickly.

Unfortunately, it came for me at the worst possible moment as it meant I could not challenge for a place in the team and not just against Jackie.

My versatility could push me down the right wing. I played international football as a centre-half and in the Celtic reserve side, I was very often to be found patrolling midfield and getting forward to score goals.

I felt that I offered the manager options that perhaps others could not, so, once I had returned from injury, I threw myself back into training, working as hard, if not harder than ever.

Frank Connor welcomed me back to the reserve side and worked on my game. He was still Frank – still with the words of encouragement – and still with the same belief in my ability which he expressed in his salty, west of Scotland voice peppered with oaths and curses.

Frank was of good, working-class stock, recognised a grafter when he saw one and could lavish praise on you like a father to his son.

He kept telling me I would be back in Tommy's plans and to keep maintaining my standards, but as far as I could see, it was to no avail. Something was happening. There was something in the atmosphere around the club that you couldn't see, but to me, it was tangible.

I felt that I was being frozen out – that's the only way I can describe it.

Nobody said anything explicit to me. Nothing about my situation or that I was not in the thoughts of Tommy Burns, but I could sense it.

I wondered if there was a disadvantage in the fact that I was not really part of the social fabric of the club.

My team-mates were good boys and we all got on well. There would always be the odd tension, of course. That was understandable. We were all healthy young men, jockeying for our position in the team and that competition for places could provide skirmishes, but on the whole, it was a happy workforce.

And yet, I believe the fact that I was not one for going out much to nightclubs and drinking like most of the boys was something that counted against me.

Having said that, I did go out one night close to Christmas to the locally famous Hamilton Palace nightclub. My brother Aleks was with me as he was staying at my house at that time.

It was his idea, but I went along anyway.

I liked the Palace. It was a busy place that attracted a very mixed clientele. I never had any trouble in the bar even though I played for one of Glasgow's big two teams. There was a respect around the place, and I felt relaxed there.

On this particular night, there was a girl who caught my eye.

I would come to realise later that she was the manageress of a branch of a successful hairdressing franchise known as 'Yours Faithfully'.

Annfrances Murray was more than a manageress. She was one of the busiest and most successful hairdressers in the franchise.

On that night, in December 1995, she was on a works outing with her colleagues and, as she tells it, was counselling one of her younger members of staff, who was going through a relationship break-up.

However, as I say, she caught my eye and, at the earliest opportunity, as she passed the bar, I offered to buy her a drink. She would tell me later that she recognised my face but was not sure from where, but coming from a family who were pretty much all daft on Celtic, that may have been a distraction.

We fell into conversation, and she asked what I did for a living.

'I am a footballer,' I replied.

And then, the key question, especially in the west of Scotland.

'Who do you play for?' she asked.

'Who do you support?' I asked, cheekily.

She looked me up and down a bit before answering. 'Celtic.'

Ha!

'I **play** for Celtic. My name is Rudi Vata.'

'You've been to my house,' she announced, which took me a bit by surprise as I was fairly certain I would have remembered both her and her house.

I laughed but I must have looked a little perplexed.

'I'm big Neily's daughter,' she continued.

Ah, now the message sank in to me.

I had been going to a local gym for a while now, in addition to the training I was doing at the club.

It was a small, well-run place where I could do some weights and work out a bit. I had even participated in five-a-side football when a few guys asked me if I could play.

You wouldn't get away with that now at a top club. In fact, I'm not even sure I would have got away with it *then* – I just didn't tell Celtic about it!

It was a guy called Tommy Dougan who asked me to play, and it became a semi-regular occurrence.

Big Neily was a goalkeeper in the opposite team, so I got to know him reasonably well.

Tommy asked me if I could get something signed for big Neily which I was happy to do and so, one night when he was driving me home, he announced that he wanted to stop at his friend's place to drop it in.

He did so but I just sat out in the car waiting for him to come back and the hedges were pretty tall in that garden so I would have been anonymous anyway!

It was big Neily's house.

This young lady was right.

I had been to her house although I had never been in it.

We talked a lot that night and, for an Albanian a long way from home and a west-of-Scotland girl with deep Scots Irish heritage, we identified with each other closely.

I would come to know that Annfrances valued my love of family, roots and a sense of where you come from and, of course, I like that about her as well.

Family.

The sense of belonging.

The blood ties that can bind people together.

We both knew and appreciated these factors.

In my life I have never regretted offering to buy a drink for Annfrances Murray – the girl who would go on to be my wife and mother to our two boys!

Our relationship started on the basis that I had sat outside her house in Tommy Dougan's car, and it continues to this day.

My new relationship was a bright spot in my personal life at a time when my professional life was not quite so happy.

As I mentioned, no one had told me that I was coming to the end of my time at Celtic, but I could sense the change in the currents of the water.

This was the way of the politics of the game. We did not have a large squad, but the matchday only accounted for a certain number of players out on the pitch and on the bench. If you were not one of them, then it was reserve team football.

I made myself available to Frank Connor and that big-hearted man kept on at me to be patient, but as the season headed to a conclusion, it was clear that I was not going to be playing first-team football.

For the record, the boys lost only one league match all season and that was the game against Rangers that I played in. However, a tendency for too many drawn matches saw points dropped and the title went, once again, across the city.

Rangers, who had already put Celtic out of the Scottish League Cup, repeated the feat in the Scottish Cup semi-final and so it was another barren season for the club.

I was out of contract in the summer, and I needed to think about my future.

Celtic set up a meeting for me with Southend United as two of my former team-mates, Paul Byrne and Mark McNally, were already there.

I went down to see the club and chat with their manager, former Liverpool and Republic of Ireland player Ronnie Whelan, but it was a bit like Brighton in so far as I knew it wasn't the place for me to be.

It just didn't feel like the best fit.

I returned to Celtic, and it was now June of 1996.

Technically, I was still a member of the first-team squad, but I was feeling remote from that group of players although there was an odd incident at the time which, I think, remained in the memories of quite a few who were around the club in those days.

Celtic had taken on a new head of athletic performance. His name was Jim Henry and he was a former Scottish title-winning judo champion.

He would go on to work at a number of clubs, including Rangers, but at that point, he was on Celtic's books and was part of the new breed of conditioning specialists that football operations were starting to employ.

Jim was a walking advert for fitness with his supremely sculpted body and, in my opinion, he handled himself with a fair degree of self-confidence that naturally comes from someone who has invested time and discipline into attaining physical perfection.

For my part, I knew nothing about judo, but since my childhood growing up in Albania, I had been more than proficient at Greco-Roman wrestling.

Aleks and I had been nurtured in this specialist category and I had competed all over the country from an early age.

Its style derived from as far back as the ancient Greek Olympics and, even today, is still a participation sport in the modern Games.

It differentiates from other freestyle wrestling in that it forbids 'holds' below the waist and is constructed on the principle of 'throws' that one can invoke on an opponent.

Celtic physiotherapist Brian Scott took an interest in it and he and I had discussed it on many an occasion while I was at the club. One day, while all the other players and I were sitting in the lounge after lunch, he mischievously asked, in front of everybody, if I would dare to wrestle Jim?

This, of course, was asked in the presence of the man himself and, as a challenge to both of us, could not be dismissed.

Jim and I looked at each other and, perhaps seeing to establish some credentials and kudos in his new workplace, he announced that he would 'put me down in 10 seconds'.

I couldn't and, indeed, *wouldn't* walk away from this challenge so I just shrugged my shoulders, and we made our way out into the foyer between the lounge and the dressing rooms.

In those days, the offices were close to this area and, as is usual, the grapevine resounded that Jim, and I were about to 'square off'.

We were both in our 'civvies', as they say, which for me was essentially a jumper and jeans.

I had absolutely no idea about how judo worked although I had heard the term for this ancient Japanese method of combat.

A crowd was beginning to form as we circled each other waiting for either of us to make a move.

I was surprised at the speed of Jim's motion as he moved towards me, and we grappled.

As we did so, he grabbed my jumper, took leverage, flipped me over and, indeed, had me pinned to the floor within those ten seconds.

Wow! The speed of it all. The way he flipped me over his right foot! Jim had moved fast to gain the advantage over me.

Ah, now I understood.

Greco-Roman wrestling is conducted with a bare upper torso so there is no facility for grabbing an opponent's clothing and using it as a tool.

I had to gain parity so, when Jim released me, I stood up and pulled my jumper up and over my head.

Now we were in *my* territory.

I had no clothing to grab.

If Jim was to take me down, he would have to do it in Greco-Roman style.

The fact that he could no longer grab an item of my clothing and was reliant on trying to grab my flesh would now work in my favour and so we wrestled in the ancient style.

I was in my element and now started to lift Jim up and throw him around the room – a few times!

As I recall, we ended up pinned to the floor, but he was unable to move from underneath me.

It was a match of different disciplines, and the early civilisation technique of Greco-Roman wrestling had the beating of the relatively newer martial art of Japanese judo.

Of course, there could be an argument that Jim was wary of injuring me as that would not have read so well for him. Just in the door as a conditioning coach and laying one of the first-team squad out with an injury … not good!

However, I felt we were evenly matched in the contest, and nobody could deny that Jim was in perfect physical shape.

About three years after this bout, I happened to be back in Glasgow on a trip. I had developed an ankle injury playing out in

Germany and, although I had not been a Celtic player for a few years, I knew that I could call upon my old friend Brian Scott for advice and treatment.

Henrik Larsson had just sustained a horrific leg break in a European game out in France that would virtually end his season at an early point and he it was who was up on the treatment table as Brian ministered to him.

I was introduced to Henrik and was hugely surprised when even the Swede immediately recounted the story of me throwing the ex-Scottish judo champion around the lounge at Celtic Park.

Clearly the legend of it all still remained!!

Incidentally, as I entered Celtic Park that day, I saw Jim, but I felt that he avoided me. Perhaps he did not want a rematch!

A super guy and, of course, coming from a disciplined fitness background myself, I always respected those who looked after their conditioning with rigidity.

Back in those days, there were not that many agents representing players in the Scottish game, but I was contacted by a Greek businessman who had handled quite a few of my Albanian team-mates, taking them over to various European countries.

His name was Paskal Papadopoulos and he owned a respected agency called PPA World. It still runs to this day, representing players from the Czech Republic, Cyprus, Bulgaria, Greece and more. He told me about an evolving situation at Greek giants, AEK Athens.

Stelios Manolas was the epitome of a one-club man, having spent his entire professional career with AEK from 1979 onwards. He had also come through their youth academy as a boy so his bond with the club was a strong one.

Popularly regarded as one of the best defenders of his era in Greek football and a natural leader out on the pitch, his influence was huge within the club and at international level.

However, by 1996, he was approaching 35 years of age and, according to Mr Papadopoulos, was ready to retire from the game. I was being touted as his replacement at the club although I did not really know that at the time.

There was also interest in me from Olympique Marseille and that held genuine appeal for me as I enjoyed my first period in France, but Paskal gave me the impression that AEK would be my next destination.

He flew me over to Greece in June of 1996 and put me up in a beautiful hotel in a place called Glyfada in the Athens Riviera area.

The hotel was first class, the weather hot and the beaches stunning but I just sat in my hotel for two whole weeks, kicking my heels whilst Paskal was handling arrangements.

I felt I could play my football here. It was a complete change of landscape, culture and climate from Glasgow, but I believed it was in my DNA to travel the world and play the game.

I was a professional footballer who had played for one of the biggest club sides in the world, so I was not particularly fazed by the prospect of coming to Greece, but there was the wrench of leaving Celtic.

I must be honest when I say that I was badly hurt by how I had been treated in what was to be my final season for the club.

Frozen out of the set-up and desperate to play for the first team, I struggled to accept the situation.

I can only describe it as an emptiness of the soul. It wasn't just the football; it was the club itself and their magnificent support.

My final game had been that European leg against Paris Saint-Germain way back in November. It would have been nice to go out on a high.

Celtic Park was always a special place to be on a big European night and probably is even more so today.

That night against PSG, there was still construction work being done on a section behind one of the goals and it was uninhabited. Yet, the noise from the rest of the ground would have suggested a full house.

That was typical of the Celtic support. Their backing for the players and the club was expressed vocally and passionately.

To be under the lights on those nights, playing against some of the best players on the continent and with that crackle in the air was a delicious sensation.

It is true what they say. You have to live in those moments.

Enjoy them.

Docket them.

Remember them.

My Celtic career was drawing to a close.

I had the satisfaction of knowing that I had, certainly for a period, proven Tommy Burns wrong in his initial and, in my opinion, hasty assessment of me and what I could bring to his squad.

Through sheer endeavour, hard work and single-mindedness, I had endured, and I had a Scottish Cup medal to prove it.

Don't believe what they tell you. You don't win anything by chance. It has to be earned and I really earned that medal to become that first Albanian footballer to win a major domestic trophy in a European league.

And then there was that support.

I knew that I could have looked every single one of them in the eye and dared them to say to me that they had not seen an honest professional who was willing to go that extra mile for them.

I could honestly say that I had worked hard in sometimes very trying circumstances to represent them, their values and the ethos of what they believed their club and a Celtic player should be.

And now it was at an end.

And I was heartbroken.

Heartbroken.

****

So, I sat in a Greek hotel waiting for my immediate future to be sorted out. Would it be AEK or Olympique Marseille for Rudi Vata?

As it turned out, it was neither.

Quite abruptly, after that fortnight of almost glamorous house arrest, Paskal Papadopoulos informed me that the deal with AEK was off.

Stelios Manolas had changed his mind about retirement and wanted to play on for another season.

In addition, the interest from Olympique Marseille appeared to have cooled as well. Probably because they had been made to wait around for some kind of response.

So, where was I going to go?

Actually, not that far from Greece.

I was being signed up to Apollon Limassol in Cyprus.

## CHAPTER 13
# CYPRUS

The world of football is certainly a different place now.

As an agent myself, I understand how it works from that perspective and players have so much more leverage than they did in my time.

Did I want to go and play in Cyprus? No.

Did I want to leave Celtic? Emphatically, no!

However, I was in the hands of Paskal Papadopoulos, and he dictated the agenda.

I was 27 years of age and, as popular surmises go, I was entering the peak of my playing career.

The move had to be right for me and I was not sure that Limassol was the place to be. However, Paskal assured me that this was the right move, and I agreed to it.

From the very first start, I had no doubts.

Limassol, like most of Cyprus, was very beautiful.

I arrived in the summer when the temperatures were peaking. The sun was a constant. Beautiful beaches, clear blue water and a climate that would have been the envy of many. It was, I suppose, a paradise.

But I had *left* 'Paradise' to be there.

Listen. I am a fighter.

I know what I have to do and back then it was clear what my job was – I had to get into the first team and be successful.

When Annfrances and I arrived in the country, we were taken for dinner by two of the club directors and I had my first real taste of Cyprus.

When I looked around at all the tourists in shorts, bikinis, tee-shirts, sunglasses and roaming around the place lapping up the weather, I came to the conclusion that this was not a football country, it was more of a holiday resort.

The question now was, could this work for me?

There is no doubt that it took me quite some time to get over leaving Celtic.

It wasn't just the stature of the club. It was the people; the support and a sense of camaraderie with them all.

In addition, I felt that the way I had been discarded had been cold, brutal almost, and that these wounds would take a long time to heal.

Still, I had a living to earn, and I have to say that I was surprised with the wage that I was receiving from Apollon.

You may also be surprised to know that, in one season at Limassol, I earned more in salary than the combined wages I had earned at Celtic in four years!

In saying that, though, if Celtic had offered me a new contract on even a modest increase, then I would willingly have committed myself to them once more.

The signing-on fee alone from Apollon was enough to allow me to buy my house in Hamilton outright and operate without a mortgage.

When I approached the bank, who held my mortgage about this matter, I was surprised when I was told that I would have to pay more than the final figure to take me out of my mortgage.

I had never heard of the penalty clause before which came into practice with an early clearing of the debt.

Still, I paid it.

What a feeling that was!

I now owned my house outright at the age of 27.

Yes, yes, I know that a lot of my contemporary players did so and I would come to realise that modern players did not even bother with mortgages, but here I was, an Albanian migrant who grew up with dreams and fantasies about having somewhere of my own and yet, doing so through the auspices of the communist regime.

My parents could never have conceived of this for themselves. It was a lifetime of servitude to the Party, the machinations of a society that put a roof over your head but crushed any ambition that you may have had to be a property owner.

My own father started his working life as a procurer of housing loans for his compatriots through the Bank of Albania and knew full well the strictures put upon those individuals who funnelled their meagre income into the bricks and mortar of their existence.

And here was I, the son of Pjeter Vata, at 27 years of age, mortgage-free and the owner of my house, my freedom and my future. The owner of myself.

It was always enough to make me grateful for my upbringing and the values instilled in me by my parents.

My brother Aleks had moved to Scotland, and he would now live in my house in Hamilton while I headed to the eastern Mediterranean to further my career.

It was another twist in the tale of my life.

And I was not going alone.

My relationship with Annfrances was secure enough for me to suggest the idea of her leaving home to come out to Cyprus.

There were quite a few hurdles to overcome in this endeavour.

As I mentioned earlier, she was extremely successful as a manageress/stylist in the Yours Faithfully salon group.

She was 23 years of age and had been with the company since apprenticeship at 16. The company had backed her, trained her and through hard work and talent, she had progressed to a great position with the promise of so much more to come in the pipeline.

The career of a hairdresser is based upon the fidelity of a clientele. One builds up a loyal customer base and sets the stall out for a business of repetitive, return visits.

To leave that position, even for a single year, is to gamble with that fidelity. Clients move on, find another stylist and, invariably, should you return to that environment, then you are effectively starting from scratch again.

I probably did not appreciate that at the time with Annfrances. My business was football, not hairdressing.

However, I fully understood the more powerful motivational factor of her familial ties.

The youngest daughter of Neily and Ann Murray, alongside sister Eileen, Clare, and Margaret-Ann and the baby of the family, Neil, she had a strong, natural bond with her entire family.

She still lived at home in Wishaw, near Glasgow, and hadn't shown any particular interest in changing that arrangement.

I could appreciate the change of this Albanian football player coming into her life, asking her to give up her career and family to travel out to an unknown part of the world and the unpredictability of a new career.

I knew what it was to leave one's home.

That was a tough choice to make, but in the six short months we had been together, I felt sure in my heart that I wanted her to be with me. She would tell me later that she crept into her mum's bedroom one night to tell her, tearfully, that she was going to Cyprus with me.

*Rudi has asked me to go with him and I said that I will,* as she put it.

It would only be in the fullness of time that Annfrances would learn that her mother was heartbroken, but in the true spirit of parenthood, she had told her that she was happy for her youngest daughter to follow *her* heart.

Neily, as I recall, was not so accommodating.

He did wonder why Annfrances was willing to leave her beloved home country and move to the middle of Europe, but crucially, he did not offer any resistance.

And so, I was set for the next part of my life, but this time, I was going with my partner.

Another adventure was beginning.

Everything about Cyprus was different from what I had ever experienced in my football career before that period.

The heat was definitely a major factor. When I reported for pre-season training, I had to do so at five o'clock in the morning.

That was the time when the island was cool enough to accommodate physical exercise. We trained until 7am and then came back at 7.30pm to work out again.

Either way, I soon learned what it meant to be a professional footballer in Cyprus.

You sweat.

You sweat a lot and, as a compensation, you had to drink gallons of water to make up for the fluid deposits in your system.

I worked hard, of course.

That was my way – the Rudi way.

There were benefits, however, to the early starts to training as it gave one the chance to enjoy the rest of the day up until training at night.

Your lifestyle was dictated by the climate and, as we had taken an apartment close to the beach, Annfrances and I were spending just about every weekend down by the shores of the Mediterranean sea.

I had been warned by a few friends that the constant sun and heat could furnish a laziness in me, but I was determined that this would not be the case.

I worked as hard in training as any of my contemporaries, if not more so.

We adapted quickly to the Cypriot lifestyle, but Annfrances did not want to live the pampered lifestyle of all play and no work.

That was not her way.

I suppose her grounding in the working-class life that she had been raised in, as had I, was a major factor.

She needed to be in the workplace and practising her hairdressing skills, so we opened up Vata Vision as a hair salon in Limassol. Here, now, was a whole new experience for Annfrances and she relished it.

For the first time in her life, she was in control of her own business, her own destiny.

What a heady feeling for her and what freedom.

Of course, running a hairdressing business in that kind of climate was completely different from Lanarkshire, Scotland.

She had the freedom to come and go as she pleased which, given the fantastic climate, meant she could enjoy the lifestyle fully.

We had a luxurious apartment, close to the action and, as I said, close to the beach.

There was, I think, only one occasion when she may have had cause to think that this was a mistake.

I was out in Albania with the international team preparing for a match when she phoned me.

*There's been an earthquake here!* she shouted down the line.

As Annfrances told me, she had been working in the salon when she experienced something that she thought was a train going past the building.

A terrific rumble followed, the building began to shake and, as she recalled, all the shampoo bottles fell off their glass shelves as the shelves started to splinter. She and the young girls who worked with her raced out into the street, keeping an eye out for any potential overhead destruction.

It must have been a terrifying experience for her and the girls.

Annfrances told me that, after the quake, the girls wanted to go back to their families, which was understandable, so she locked up the salon and headed back to our apartment.

The surround at the door had moved in the tremor and she could smell the reek of alcohol because, clearly, the bottles that we had in our bar area had all fallen off the shelf, smashing on to the floor.

Even now, as she called me, she could feel the aftershock which was an experience quite unlike any other she had had in her life. I was a bit more used to earthquakes as a boy as Albania had quite a few but to Annfrances this was something frightening and new.

After calling me and calming down, she went straight to the house of a friend from Edinburgh who had married a Cypriot and was living there. She gave her a bed for the night.

So, yes, that might have been a moment when she mused over her decision to re-locate to Cyprus, but as I will recall later, it was not her last earthquake.

* * *

I was beginning to enjoy my football again and had arrived at the club at the same time as my new manager.

Momcilo 'Moka' Vukotic was Serbian and as a player had enjoyed success with FK Partizan of the former Yugoslavia as well as being capped by his nation. He had been coaching in Cyprus for about six years when he arrived at Limassol, and he would eventually go on to be coach of the Cypriot national team.

I found him to be a fair guy in his approach to his players. He was willing to give every one of us a sporting chance to show what we could do.

I felt, in the time that I was with him, that I improved my tactical brain. He had a way of making you think about the game; the way it unfolded out on the pitch and, naturally, I improved as a result of his counsel.

As I said, he was Serbian, and I was Albanian. Even though he had earned his living in Cyprus for a few years, we were still regarded as outsiders.

At the time, there was a ruling in European football that a club could only field three foreign players.

In that respect, I was joined by another Serbian, Vojislav Budimirovic, who was a striker and had also played in the Bulgarian league as well as his home country.

Milenko Spoljaric, another forward and Croatian, had been at Apollon for four years when I arrived and not only would he remain at the club for a full 11 seasons, but he would also, despite his heritage, go on to play internationally for Cyprus.

The hegemony at Apollon Limassol was very clear to me. As the three foreign players at the club, we were expected to be the best players in the side.

In that respect, we were on far higher wages than our Cypriot team-mates. In some instances, three times as much, but that salary brought the obvious pressures with it.

Basically, if it was all going wrong, we would be the subject of the fans' ire and, believe me, the support was intense and passionate.

I had been used to crowds upwards of 40,000 at Celtic Park, particularly on a big European night. In my time there, as you know, Fergus McCann undertook a complete reconstruction of the stadium which made it a magnificently large arena in which to play your football.

The Tsirio Stadium in Limassol, which we shared with other senior sides, AEL Limassol and Aris Limassol, had a capacity of just over 13,000, but with a full house, you could feel the crowd bearing down on you.

That was fine by me. In fact, I thrived on it. They had a right to express their views and, as I said, my foreign team-mates and I had to match their expectations as well as our salaries.

As always, I was never, ever going to let any supporter of any club with which I played accuse me of not giving my all to the cause, in training as much as out on the pitch.

Mentality was the key to this, as in so many things.

I felt that the Albanian mentality was on a par with the Cypriot/Greek mind processes.

We understood hard work and graft, working in the knowledge that it was the only way to get our just rewards.

I respected my team-mates, of course, although that is not always a given, but they were a good bunch of honest professionals.

I believe they saw myself, Milenko and Vojislav as the saviours of their side and we all worked well together.

We had a good season that year although we finished 13 points behind the eventual champions, Anorthosis, in second place.

That, however, had been better than the mid-table finishes of the previous two seasons and meant that we were automatically in the first qualifying round of the UEFA Cup.

Intriguingly, Celtic were as well and, of course, your mind wanders to the possibilities of an encounter, but in the end, we were drawn against the Finnish side MyPa.

Finland.

The very mention of the country took me straight back to 1987 when Vllaznia Shkoder were down to play FK RoPS in that second leg tie out in Scandinavia.

This was the dangerous time in my life when my good friend and team-mate, Faslli Fakja, was not allowed to travel.

When I myself was taken to the airport but not allowed to get on the aeroplane for some reason.

And, of course, when two more of my team-mates, Arvid Hoxha and Luli Bershemi, sought asylum on the way back and that stopover in Athens.

That meeting with the *Sigurimi* in the Rofaza Hotel, Shkoder when it was made clear to me that they felt there was another traitor in the room.

Within days, I was plummeted into that world of hostility and suspicion, marked out as an 18-year-old boy with ambition with a father who was being whispered about as a spy for the Yugoslavians.

It had taken a sheet of paper and the signature of the powerful Hekuran Isai to guarantee my safety and that of my family.

Ten years.

Ten years when so much had changed for my country and, of course, for Rudi Vata.

At 28, I was in charge of my own destiny.

This time, I knew I would be flying out to Finland as a free individual and all I would have to concentrate on was my football.

Out in Anjalankoski, it took an 86th-minute equaliser from our Cypriot striker Angelos Tsolakis to secure us a 1-1 draw and provide an away goal to take back to Limassol.

However, we did not need that as three second-half goals took us through to the second qualifying round and a match against the Belgian side, Excelsior Mouscron.

They were a harder proposition and we failed to break them down at home in a 0-0 draw. Unfortunately, a 3-0 defeat in Belgium knocked us out of the competition.

A third-place finish in the league meant that the club could compete once again in the UEFA Cup the following season, but we were already guaranteed a place in the European Cup Winners' Cup as we made our way through to the Cypriot Cup Final and were facing Anorthosis Famagusta, who had retained their league title from the previous season.

They would automatically qualify for the UEFA Champions League so we would represent Cyprus in the now-defunct cup competition.

Of course, the last time that I had played in a national cup final was for Celtic three years before in that match against Airdrieonians at Hampden.

I have already explained the pressure going into that one given the barren seasons before, but equally, Celtic usually went into a final as favourites. However, that was not the case for Apollon Limassol in the 1998 Cypriot Cup Final.

Anorthosis, at the time, were the rich boys in Cyprus. They had the budget to match their ambitions, would go on to be the first Cypriot team to play in the UEFA Champions League group stages and are still regarded as one of the most successful teams in the country. We all knew we were in for a game against the champions and so it proved to be.

In saying that, we held our own for some considerable time after pulling back an equaliser just before the break, but a couple of late goals was enough to see us lose out.

Naturally, I was disappointed. It would have been nice to add another cup medal to the one I picked up in Scotland, but that's football.

We had given a good account of ourselves and at least I could be happy with my own performance.

However, there was more to it than that – I knew it would be my last game for the club.

It had been a wonderful two years and certainly much better than I had perhaps anticipated when I first arrived at the club, but now it was time once again to move on and I was excited by the new challenge.

## CHAPTER 14

# *EINE NEUE AUFGABE* (A NEW CHALLENGE)

If there is a theme to some of my movements around the world of football to various clubs, then it is linked to the international game.

Liam Brady first saw me out on the pitch in that fateful match against the Republic of Ireland in 1992 and, on the strength of that performance, he took me to Glasgow and Celtic.

A similar performance against *Northern* Ireland out in Zurich in a World Cup qualifier from September of 1997 attracted the interest of Guy Mathez, who was about to be installed as the manager of FC Basel of Switzerland.

Why Zurich? Well, Albania was at its height of the civil unrest and disorder that I have written about previously. The army had lost control of the streets and guns were plentiful but in the hands of the wrong people. You may recall from earlier, how I wrote about the shooting of my friend, Blenard Hasami, in Berat as he was involved in a situation way over his head.

That was typical of the time. The government were trying to enforce a 9pm curfew right across the country, but hey, if you are out in the streets after that hour, and you have a gun in your hand, who is there to stop you?

It was a period when I feared for my parents, but they had seen it all in their lives and would keep their heads down as all raged around them.

Under the circumstances though, FIFA and UEFA took the joint decision that it would be impossible for European and international fixtures to be played in Albania as security could not be guaranteed.

Thankfully, it has been the only campaign to date when we were required to play our home fixtures at neutral grounds in Europe. That is why we were in Zurich to play against Northern Ireland.

Albania beat the Irish that night, 1-0, in a result that undoubtedly resounded around Europe. A goal from Altin Haxhi in the 65th minute was enough to take what we felt was a significant step forward in our international progress.

This was a good Irish side that featured, among others, exciting Newcastle United winger Keith Gillespie, the experienced striker Iain Dowie, then at West Ham United, and future Celtic midfielder and manager, Neil Lennon.

Nobody expected us to win the game, but let me assure you, we were worthy of that win.

Mathez took over at Basel the following January and he made overtures to me about moving to Switzerland as my contract was due to expire in the summer.

If I recall correctly, he even came to watch me play in that Cypriot Cup Final against Anorthosis Famagusta.

It would be fair to say he was keen on me and I, in turn, was ready for a new challenge in another country.

I had enjoyed a good final season in Cyprus, to the extent that I was named as the Foreigner of the Year and for the national team as captain the newspapers were calling me the 'Beckenbauer of Albania'.

That, of course, was quite an accolade and, although I did not model my football style on 'Der Kaiser', it was apparent that I had been given a similar role for my country to the one that the great German player had employed throughout his career.

My job was not just to defend but to bring the ball out of that defence and into midfield from where I might be able to orchestrate attacks and influence the play.

They call it *libero,* literally, 'free'. Free to come out and play and it was another stage of my football development that could possibly now take me to Switzerland.

However, there was another international match, in October of 1997, that not only brought me under more scrutiny, but, on the back of the Northen Ireland result the previous month, also raised the stock of the whole Albanian national team.

It was out in Hannover against Germany.

The Germans were managed by former World Cup winner Berti Vogts and could boast the creative genius of midfielder Andreas Moller, experienced Bayern Munich goalkeeper Oliver Kahn and the firepower of Oliver Bierhoff up front who, at that point was a top striker in Italy's Serie A.

In addition, they were also the current European champions, a Bierhoff goal winning the 1996 final against the Czech Republic. In short, they were a formidable outfit, and we were facing them in front of 45,000 partisan Germans in the Heinz Von Heiden Arena. We knew instinctively that we could give them a game, however, as we had matched them well in a previous encounter earlier that year, out in Granada.

We had even taken the lead on the hour mark through a Bledar Kola penalty kick, but the Germans rallied to equalise three minutes later courtesy of an Ulf Kirsten goal before the same player added two more for a hat-trick in the final ten minutes.

We weren't finished though and when Kola scored another penalty in the 90th minute, I was certain we had the away side worried for the remaining minutes of the match.

Not only had we given our best against the European champions, but we had also shown them that we could and would compete right up until the final whistle.

Our manager Astrit Hafizi had instilled in us a tough mentality and a willing collectiveness to represent our country in a respectful manner. Still, I am sure the Germans would have been supremely confident for the return fixture on their own soil.

Once again, though, we matched up to them in Hannover and, just like the previous encounter, we took the lead close to the hour when a cross from Alban Bushi into the box was met by a misguided header from defender and captain Jurgen Kohler which, instead of floating into the arms of Oliver Kahn, rocketed into the net.

Again, the hosts came back quickly when a near-post header from Thomas Helmer drew them level and they then took the lead ten minutes later when that man Bierhoff got his head on to a cross from six yards out.

It was now our turn to roar back when Igli Tare stole in between two German defenders and produced a beautiful finish to tie us at two apiece with ten minutes left to play.

One of our boys got caught on the bal moments later in the right-back position and, from the subsequent cross, substitute Olaf Marschall slid in to make it 3-2.

This was the painful lesson of football at this elite level – you can get punished with the smallest disregard for detail.

Possibly, the German players and, indeed, the crowd thought that it was over at that point, but perhaps they had not considered our dogged mentality to keep on going.

I will address my entire international career in a subsequent chapter, but it is sufficient to say that one of the most memorable moments in that career unfolded in the 87th minute that night in Hannover.

From a short corner kick, we made our way into the German box. Bledar Kola attempted a shot that ricocheted off a defender before falling just in front of me, about eight yards out. I quickly adjusted my feet and cracked a low drive past Oliver Kahn and into the corner of the net.

What a feeling!

We had a small but loyal band of Albanian supporters in a special section of the stadium and they erupted with pleasure at the equaliser.

Yes, indeed, it was one of the sweetest moments in my life as well as my career.

Here we were now, drawing 3-3, away from home and giving the European champions a real fright.

I remember gesturing to my team-mates to keep running, keep working and let's see the match out for a famous draw or, perhaps, even grab a winner.

Sadly, it was not to be.

In the 90th minute, the ghost of Bierhoff came back to haunt us as he once again fastened on to a cross and headed cleanly and convincingly beyond Foto Strakosha in our goal to give the Germans a 4-3 victory.

The classic football moment of so near and yet so far.

It was not a national disgrace to lose to the European champions, but I do not doubt that Bierhoff's winner was met more with relief than joy by the Germans.

We had given them a game and, as I wrote earlier, left 'nothing out on the pitch'.

I had no doubt that our performances were making Europe look at the Albanian national side in a different light.

Certainly, one man who was taking an interest was Eduard Geyer, the coach of Bundesliga 2 side FC Energie Cottbus.

Just like Guy Mathez, he had seen me play, especially in that match out in Hannover, and he had decided to bring me to Germany for the next phase of my career.

I was flattered about the attention of the two managers but wasn't sure about the quality of Swiss football. I consulted a couple of my national team-mates who played in the country, and they basically told me that the standard, even in the second tier of the German Bundesliga, was higher at that time than the standard of the Swiss domestic scene.

If I am to be completely honest, I did feel that German football would be more suited to my outlook and personality.

I suspected even then that this would be a great challenge but one that I would relish and so I committed to the Bundesliga 2 side.

In Eduard Geyer, I encountered a manager unlike any other I had worked with previously.

He had been born in Bielsko, Poland towards the end of World War II when the German army still occupied the country.

After the war, his family fled to Dresden and what would become, in that post-war period, East Germany.

One can only imagine what the Geyer family discovered in that husk of a city that had infamously been attacked by Allied bombing raids in the early part of 1945.

Geyer would have grown up, quite literally, on a bomb site and among a people under the auspices of Soviet occupation.

Like me, he had grown up under communist rule, although I could argue that they were two differing strains of oppression.

Different totalitarian regimes apply their own methods of control and fashion their own brands of governance.

Whatever, it is entirely possible that this is where he honed his devotion to discipline and hard work as well as a tongue that spoke what his mind thought. Over the years, particularly as a manager, he would garner a reputation for speaking his mind freely and without regret.

A lot of his contemporaries would 'play the game' with sports journalists but this was not Geyer's style.

I felt that he was forthright, honest and would not tolerate any deviation from those assets.

When I signed from Energie Cottbus, there was a headline in one of the newspapers announcing that the club had landed the 'Beckenbauer of Albania'. The title was following me from those performances against Germany in the qualifiers.

I never paid any attention to 'paper talk' but Eduard Geyer may have thought that I did and so, just after I joined the club, he called me into his office.

He was very deliberate with me, choosing his words carefully.

'Young man,' he said, 'you may be the Beckenbauer in *your* country, but we already have only *one* Beckenbauer in Germany. You must demonstrate to me exactly who you are and how you will fit into my team.'

I accepted his words and appreciated the honest way in which he had spoken to me.

Of course, I would have to earn his respect and that of my team-mates if I was to survive and flourish in this new environment.

Geyer had been the last official manager of the Deutsche Demokratische Republic (German Democratic Republic) national side before German reunification in 1990.

He was a hard-bitten character, and I would have described him as more of a motivational manager than an overall tactician.

As I said, he believed in discipline and hard work as the basic tools for advancement and he used them to great effect in the Cottbus dressing room.

The standard in Bundesliga 2 was among some of the best I had encountered in my career.

The club was all-encompassing to the point of furnishing Annfrances and me with a lavish four-bedroom villa and a car. Remarkably, they took care of all our utility bills as well.

In addition, the salary was the best I had in my time in the game with a sometimes-astonishing win bonus for the big games.

Of course, one had to earn the riches with hard work.

The club would weigh you in the pre-season period and then set a target weight for you. If you went over that weight, you would be fined.

You would go through a complete medical from head to toe to assess every aspect of your body. I had never seen anything so thorough in that approach to health, wellbeing and fitness.

When your medical was completed, the club would send your results off to the German Football Association (DFB) in Berlin for further scrutiny.

In my case, I had to do two more tests and send them back. I assumed this was the norm but the boys in the dressing room assured me that it was not the case.

It appeared that they could not believe my results as they were on a par with heavyweight boxers and Tour de France cyclists. I had always looked after myself, but I was at my strongest and fittest in my time in Germany and it felt good.

You were expected to be a total professional, committed to the task. If you were seen at the McDonald's chain with a burger or drinking a Coca-Cola, then you would be fined.

I discovered that the country had a robust system that was equally as strict. You needed to avoid the temptation to run an amber light at the traffic lights as a camera would pick this up and you would receive an automatic fine of 100 Deutsche Marks.

The onus was clear – *you* were responsible for your own actions.

A typical day at the club would see us train from 10–12 in the morning. There would be a short break for lunch around 12.30 and then you had a chance to go home, put your feet up and relax before returning for the afternoon session.

There was another area that German clubs were adamant on – you had to learn the language.

The clubs provided a German tutor for after training on a Tuesday and Thursday and you had to attend the classes.

They saw it as an essential part of your job to integrate into the country and culture and be able to communicate, on even a rudimentary basis, with German nationals.

The club were looking after your lifestyle, living conditions and you were earning well at the very apex of that agreement, so you were expected to comply with their system.

I am not saying that I wasn't tired after the sessions and, naturally, there were times when the very last thing I wanted to do was start to concentrate on another language, but I also saw it as part of my education.

My father prized education on a higher level to the extent, as you know, that he was prepared to literally smuggle a Catholic priest into our house to teach Aleks and me a second language. He saw that as a key component of freedom and now, here I was, enjoying the fruits of all that sacrifice.

Who was I to complain about being encouraged to expand my lingual skills *and* get paid for it?

My father could never have imagined such largesse – or benevolence.

And so, I took to life in Germany, as did Annfrances.

In fact, I would go as far as saying it was one of the best decisions of my life to go to that country.

Cottbus were ambitious and everything was geared towards us climbing to the Bundesliga top tier.

We were a very cosmopolitan squad as the club recruited from all over Europe and even North America and Africa.

I was joined by players from Nigeria, Bulgaria, Hungary, Canada, Bosnia-Herzegovina, Croatia and other countries.

I think that was unusual for German football at the time and, further down the line, in April 2001 we became the first club in Bundesliga history to field an entire team of foreign players including the three substitutes. If my memory serves me right, it was against Hertha Berlin, and I was on the pitch that day along with all the other multi-national players.

The club had a history that dated back to just after the First World War, but they were banned by the Nazis in 1933 only to resurrect themselves in the post-war period under a number of names playing their football in East Germany.

In 1990, they took on the name FC Energie Cottbus after German reunification.

It could have been a factor that, as a former East German domestic team, the club had more of a point to prove when coming up against their West German counterparts, who probably had far greater resources and wealth.

I sensed a club in a hurry to get to the big stage and I intended to be very much a part of that ambitious project.

*The final whistle and Paul McStay races over to celebrate with me.*

*The wait is over as Celtic win their first major honour in six years – the Scottish Cup. With captain Paul McStay (L), I lift the old trophy above the head of Tosh McKinlay (M)*

*The first Albanian footballer to win a major domestic honour in Europe outside of his country – and I wasn't about to let the trophy go!*

*Another fashion error? I can't remember who gave me the yellow sombrero after the cup final, but I wore it anyway!*

*Kicking off the 1995/96 season with a Celtic away strip that may now be a classic!*

*1996. Annfrances and I enjoying the coast on her first ever trip to Albania.*

*Playing for Energie Cottbus. My time in Germany was the most satisfying period of my professional career.*

The irrepressible Eduard Geyer. He always spoke his mind and here he does the same with me in a match against Bayern Munich.

Energie Cottbus have just been promoted to Bundesliga 1 for the first time in their history and I celebrate in the dressing room with a team-mate and Eduard Geyer.

*Captaining my country meant shaking hands pre-match with some of the greatest leaders of their own national sides. Here it's Jurgen Klinsmann of Germany.*

*Going in hard for Albania against Germany's Dietmar Hamann in Leverkusen. Representing and captaining my country were huge honours for me.*

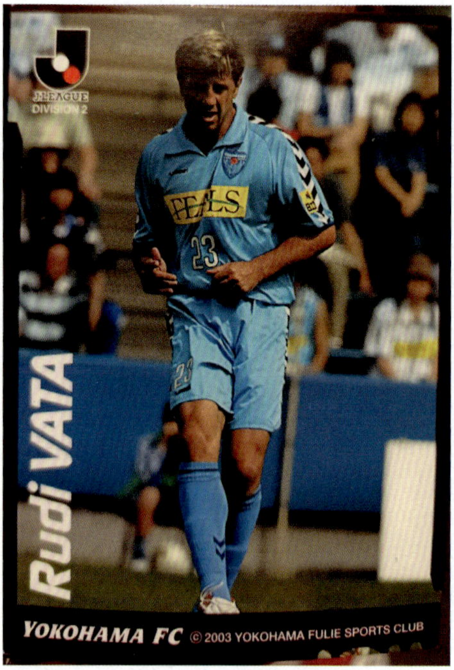


*Poster boy for Yokohama FC with blonde hair!*

*One for the scrapbook. Ruan and Rocco meet the great Lionel Messi after a 2012 UEFA Champions League match between Celtic and Barcelona. The Celts had memorably won 2-1 on the night.*

*Relaxing in Japan with Annfrances and young Ruan. Fatherhood was a great responsibility for me and Yokohama offered us so much as a family.*

2017. Still wearing the Hoops. This time for a former players' charity derby match in Ayrshire.

Ruan is more of a thinker, but he works himself hard in the gym.

A real family affair as 12-year-old Rocco signs his new contract with Celtic.

2023. Rocco makes an appearance for the Celtic first team at home to Motherwell.

*May 2024. Ruan and Rocco with his medal on the day Celtic pick up the SPFL Premiership trophy.*

*My hometown of Shkoder today. It looks very different from my youth days, but I was brought up less than 500 yards from this area.*

*July 2024. Ruan and I with Rocco on the day he signed for Watford FC.*

*Relaxing and enjoying a beer with the founder of the Albanian Celtic Supporters' Club – former national president, Ilir Meta.*

*2024 and the Vata family now.*

## CHAPTER 15

# THE BEST OF DAYS

The competition for places at Energie Cottbus was keen and it reminded me of the situation at Apollon Limassol.

You had to be better than the home-grown players to get into the side albeit there weren't that many of them in our squad of nomadic multi-nationals.

In that first season that I was at the club it felt like a period of transition, and we finished 11th in the league on 49 points. The third-placed side, SSV Ulm 1846, were on 58 points and were promoted so, with three points for a win, we were not that far off the running but knew that we had to improve the following year.

And we did.

On a personal level, the season of 1999/2000 would be one of the most memorable in my career.

Our improvement was there for all to see, and we finished third in the league behind champions FC Koln and VfL Bochum in second place.

We were now promoted to Bundesliga 1.

It was a close-run thing though, as we were only three points ahead of FC Nurnberg.

However, as they say, it doesn't matter *how* you get there – just get there!

This was massive for all the people in the city of Cottbus.

It was the first time in the club's history that they would be competing in the Bundesliga 1 and everyone wanted to celebrate the fact – even the mayor!

We were entered into *Der Goldene Buch* – literally, the Golden Book – which was, I guess, the same as being given the keys to the city.

The book was a big part of the city's heritage and to be named in its pages was a huge honour.

What a party in the streets!

It felt like a carnival in Rio de Janeiro!

The team were driven through the city centre in a convoy of soft-top cars with the roofs down.

I can only imagine that it might have been like that when Germany won the World Cup, but this seemed more personal.

An explosion of joy.

An outpouring of love for the team, the club and the city.

In football terms, FC Energie Cottbus were, finally, on the map.

It didn't matter that we had not won the Bundesliga 2. In fact, I would suggest that this was better because we had confounded all expectations except, perhaps, our own and to be a part of it was something incredibly special to me.

It was a reminder, once again, of the difference football can make to people's lives. How it can motivate them and take them to a happier place even if only for a short time.

Just like that Scottish Cup Final win with Celtic, it was important to live in the moment at such times.

Important to take it all in and savour it.

You just never know if those moments will come along again.

And for me, of course, football represented my freedom and I genuinely believe that the happiest period of my career was in Germany.

I was at my fittest and my strongest and playing with a club that had ambition.

Now, we had to work to be worthy of our place in the higher league because, as a newly promoted side, we no doubt would be installed by the media as one of the favourites to be relegated.

This would be the season when we would be up against the big names in German football. Bayer Leverkusen, Borussia Dortmund, Schalke 04 and, of course, Bayern Munich.

It would also be the season when I got to meet Der Kaiser himself – the legendary Franz Beckenbauer.

I did so when we played Bayern and, I can tell you, he oozed class.

Here was the man who was credited with developing the *libero* and, at the same time, completely modernising the role of a defensive sweeper.

I was honoured that he knew who I was, but then again, football, German football in particular had been his lifeblood and, as club president for Bayern Munich which he was at that time, he would have been aware of who was who at the various clubs.

We actually beat Bayern that season.

Our home form, the season before in the Stadion der Freundschaft (Stadium of Friendship) had been the bedrock for our promotion and we always fancied ourselves against anyone on our own soil, so we were not intimidated by the Rolls-Royce machine coming from Munich.

Given that Bayern only lost nine games that season on their way to the title and would also go on to win the UEFA Champions League for the first time in 25 years, it was a notable achievement for us to get a 1-0 result against them.

We also added Schalke, Hertha Berlin and Hamburg to our list of conquests.

Eduard Geyer had a clear plan for us, and we fought like lions for him. As I said earlier, he was more of a motivational manager than a brilliant tactician and his ability to handle players and understand their strengths and weaknesses was a major factor in our success.

He was never afraid to speak out and he was viewed as a real character in German football.

Character. This was always a quality I looked for in people.

From my own perspective, I knew how important it was to be someone of character.

People of character stand apart from the herd and are always recognised and remembered.

My character was built upon reality, truth and survival and life has taught me that, as long as I square myself with God, and not just people, then I can survive any situation.

For me, it is important to have that relationship with the 'big guy' and sometimes in life, possibly like when I agreed to go to Cyprus, I acted against my own personal preference or interest, but as a free spirit I could be comfortable with that as I knew that I could survive any given situation.

And, of course, Germany was like that for me. Embrace the new country, the new experiences and develop as a person.

Keep my relationship with God and work hard to make sure that I could survive and flourish.

And I can tell you, working with Eduard Geyer could very often be a matter of survival.

I will never forget a game that we played against Eintracht Frankfurt in February of 2001.

FC Energie Cottbus were never a rich club and so, instead of flying across Germany to fulfil fixtures, we just used to take a bus to the games.

That was a challenge when the journey from Cottbus to Frankfurt, by coach, could take close to five hours.

It was a Friday night match as was often the case in Bundesliga 1 and the kick-off was at 8.15pm.

You knew you would be in for a tough match taking into account the travel time, late kick-off and other mitigating factors.

We had beaten our opponents back in September, 2-0 at home with goals from our Croatian striker Antun Labak and a late finish from my German team-mate Sebastian Helbig, so we knew we had the tools to do the job that night.

Eintracht were enduring a traumatic season and their manager, the famous former German internationalist, Felix Magath, had been sacked by the club at the end of January.

Ultimately, they would finish second-bottom of the table and be relegated and yet, as was sometimes the way when a new manager comes in, in this case, former journeyman midfielder, Rolf Dohmen, the team got a short bounce from the appointment.

We played well for the first hour, full of that energy, commitment and the fighting spirit that Eduard Geyer had made his hallmark at the club, but when we lost a goal on 65 minutes to German striker Horst Heldt, we appeared to be up against it.

We still had close to half an hour to get back into the match, but on a frustrating night, our performance was not up to the standards we had previously set. We were toiling rather than dominating.

I am sure we knew that.

Eduard Geyer certainly did, and he was waiting for us to unleash a tirade at full time in the dressing room.

He went absolutely crazy at us and, it has to be said, with some justification.

When you consider that we were only to finish four points ahead of Frankfurt in the table and that they, as a consequence, dropped a division, you could see how tight the margins were when it came to picking up those points.

He railed at us for some time, and then we were ordered into the showers for a quick turnaround so that we could get the coach back to Cottbus. A shower, a bite to eat and we were all back on board the bus to set off once again.

There isn't much worse than a long journey, in the dead of a dark, cold winter night back home when you have lost a football match.

And that night was no exception.

One of the rules enforced by the German authorities was that a bus driver had to stop driving after three hours and rest for a short period of time before getting back out on the road. It was a safety precaution and quite sensible, if a bit frustrating.

You can't really get a good sleep on a bus at the best of times, but with the enforced stops, the ensuing distance and the mid-winter conditions, our journey back time crept up to just over six hours.

We arrived back at Cottbus, weary, tired and really just wanting to get back to our own homes and, more importantly, our own beds.

It was now close to 5am and, along with the other wives and partners, Annfrances had risen early and was waiting for me in our car, outside the stadium.

But it wasn't to be that easy.

Eduard Geyer had clearly spent the entire journey seething about both our performance and the result.

It could have gone either way with him. The journey would have given him a chance to reflect, to work it all out and plan ahead.

Or the length of time, the enforced delays, the feeling of unfinished business could have gnawed away at him for the whole journey.

We were about to find out it was the latter.

As we disembarked the bus, he told us to go straight to the dressing room.

I didn't even get the chance to say anything to Annfrances as she sat at the wheel of the car.

Once inside, we learned it was just Part Two of the Frankfurt tirade.

Our performance was, in his words, *catastrophic*. We had *lost concentration* at vital points in the match.

And so, it continued.

We were privileged that we only had to work for two hours a day and were being handsomely paid 3,000 Deutsche Marks for this luxury.

Hundreds of good people worked much longer hours for less money than we were being handed.

The bonus system of 5,000DM for a Bundesliga win and up to 15,000DM for taking the scalps of the big clubs like Bayern Munich was much better money than the majority of the working people of Germany were earning and we were being selfish and patronising by not giving our all out on the pitch.

Once he had finished ranting, he paused and then we found out what he really had in mind.

He told us to change into our training kit and put on these specially constructed boots for running – in the snow!

We were all to go outside, 56-year-old Eduard Geyer included, and complete a 10km run around the circumference of the lake that was located just across from the stadium.

And we were warned – any player who dropped behind our manager would be fined for slacking off – and, of course, he meant it!

So, there we all were.

Ninety minutes of football on a cold February night – an elongated journey back to Cottbus that saw us arrive at 5am – and all of us fairly shattered but now being ordered to do a 10km run at pace!

I will never forget the sounds of the heavy breathing coming from our squad as the snow crunched under the soles of our boots on our run. The moon was still out and shining down on us as we made our way through the cold gloom. We could actually see the manifestation of our breath in the morning air and, all the while, you would occasionally hear the howling of the wolves who populated the forest beside the lake.

It was eerie, tough, relentless as we made damn sure none of us fell behind our manager.

Yet, we had no choice. You were like a soldier serving your country.

Eduard Geyer let us know, in his own inimitable way – this is your job. This is what you do for a living and if you are not happy about it then he would personally tear up your contract in front of you.

As I said before – he was unlike any previous manager with whom I had worked.

And yet, I have to say, I loved it.

Certainly, it was this kind of discipline, this hard work ethic that ensured we kept our place at the elite level of the German Bundesliga 1.

As I said previously, unquestionably, as the third-placed team in the promotion spots from the season before, we would have been favourites to go straight back down as a relegated side, but Eduard Geyer never saw it that way and neither did we.

Our mantra was to work hard, fight like those lions that I mentioned and surprise teams with our speed, strength and collective mindset.

Of course, there would be bumps along the road such as the disappointment in Frankfurt, but if we stuck to our principles we would prevail.

On a personal basis, it was a season when I was voted the best-sculpted body in the Bundesliga, which I felt justifiably proud about, especially at 32 years of age.

I played 32 out of the 34 games we played that season and also got selected six times in the Best Bundesliga XI by the writers of the venerable German football magazine, *Kicker*.

I was now firmly established in Germany and in the German football set-up.

Unquestionably, this was the greatest and most satisfying period of my career. My work/life balance appeared to be perfect.

Annfrances was equally happy, and we were sharing these new experiences and this fantastic lifestyle together.

As soon as the season finished, we headed off to Montenegro for a holiday. It was a chance to reset after a hard campaign, but as was my way, I wanted to maintain my fitness and get ready for the new season.

As a consequence, it became my habit to go for a run every day out on the beach. Generally, I would clock around 10km, but one day, I started to feel something like a small needle at the base of my back.

I reasoned with myself that I could run it off, but it grew more persistent.

Our pre-season training was in Vienna, Austria, but I knew there was something seriously wrong when we got there, and I could not bend my left leg. It appeared to be frozen, and the pain shot up from the point of my toe to the base of my spine.

I was diagnosed with sciatica, so I sought treatment at the earliest opportunity. What it certainly meant was that I would be missing the start of the new season until I could get back to full fitness.

I was now about to go from the best period of my career to the worst and, to be honest, tried to get back to fitness too quickly.

I should really have remembered my time at Le Mans when I forced myself to play earlier than I should have after my ankle break and almost lost my foot as a consequence, but it was the Rudi way.

The problem was that when I started to feel a bit better after the treatment from the doctor, I would push myself too hard in training which, inevitably, led to a breakdown again.

In fairness, the medical advice I was receiving told me just to work on certain aspects of my physique and not to overload on the sessions, but I was not inclined to listen.

As a professional footballer, I had strived to play through pain. The mentality feeds the physicality, but it was a bit difficult for me to accept that, my body had and was changing, and I needed to understand that change of direction.

Out on the pitch, the team had started the season badly and, given our resources as a small club, it was not easy to bulk up the squad with new players.

My contract was until the end of the season, but I was not playing first-team football apart from 45 minutes against TSV 1860 Munich. Even in that game, I felt that, at best, my fitness was only clocking in at around 70% and that was just not acceptable for me, or the team.

It was clear my recovery, rehabilitation and fitness were taking their toll and I felt that the club and, more importantly, the manager were losing faith in me.

That disappointed me immensely. I felt that I had given my all to Energie Cottbus, been a good servant to the club and was an integral part of the successes we had enjoyed together.

It was a time when I needed a bit more support and, to me, it was not there.

It seemed to come to a crisis point towards the end of December when Eduard Geyer called me on the telephone to see how I was feeling.

We were about to enter the mid-winter break which would last around two weeks and it felt like he was doing a bit of housekeeping, tying up any outstanding business or giving vent to what was on his mind following the start we had endured in the campaign to date. He quickly cut to the chase.

The club appeared to have a plan and they were looking for my agreement to it. My contract was up to the end of June, but I had my pride, and I could have made them stick to that agreement. If I was not wanted though then I, in turn, did not want to be there, but as I say, I was disappointed.

Looking back, it was probably a bit selfish of me, but I was still a young man, albeit an experienced professional.

Sometimes, footballers have that selfishness in them whereas now I can appreciate that the club is always bigger than the player or, at least, it should be that way.

In my defence, Annfrances was expecting our first child at that point, so it was not all self-interest.

I was about to become a father and ready to take on that responsibility, so the financial security and welfare of my family was also uppermost in my thoughts.

I knew there were a few Bundesliga 2 clubs expressing interest in me, and I felt I had earned that interest from my experience of playing in Germany at a high level domestically as well as being captain of the Albanian national team.

One club seemed especially keen to sign me on a deal until the end of the season and that was Leichtatletik Rasensport Ahlen or LR Ahlen as they were known at the time. They switched their name to Rot Weiss Ahlen in 2006, but when I was there, it was LR.

Ahlen was based in the west of the country close to Dortmund and the powerhouses of Dusseldorf and Cologne.

They operated in the Bundesliga 2 having just moved into that league for the first time the season before after promotion from Regionalliga West/Sudwest.

Like Cottbus, they were ambitious, and I jumped at the chance of joining the club.

I just wanted to get back to the game.

To be fair, Energie Cottbus paid out the remainder of my contract and that, coupled with the fact that I was playing for the Ahlen first team meant that I was earning a double salary so, all in all, it was a good deal.

A piece of short-term financial security and I was back playing football as well.

My fitness had improved but I was still being advised not to stretch my left leg too much and, this time, I listened to the medical team.

The club's manager at the time was a man named Uwe Rapolder. He was a big, imposing guy, standing in at 6ft 3in.

Just like Eduard Geyer, he was a character who believed in being strict and disciplined.

To be completely honest, I found him to be a little bit too serious and with more than a hint of arrogance about him.

Don't misunderstand me, arrogance can be a positive characteristic, in my opinion, but it was the type of arrogance that can be lost in translation out on a training ground or a football pitch on matchday.

He had us playing what I would call 'vertical' football, which is to say, attack-minded and getting the ball forward into the front men as quickly as possible without much creativity.

I have to be honest and say that I did not really feel that I connected with the club the way I had at Energie Cottbus.

I played, I think, about 14 games in the run-in to the end of a season when Ahlen finished mid-table and failed to get promotion.

The deal had been to the end of the campaign and now it was over.

The summer of 2002 would be one of change for Rudi Vata.

I was out of contract, without a club and, at 33 years of age, about to become a father.

CHAPTER 16

# BACK TO THE BEGINNING

I cannot truly say that I was worried about my situation in that summer of 2002 although, for the first time in my professional career, dating back to when I was 18, I found myself without a club.

Even when I left Celtic, there were still hands to be played and, of course, that led me to Cyprus and Apollon Limassol.

Still, there were people looking out for me.

People such as Fali Ramadani, who was that rarity in those days in that he was an Albanian football agent.

He lived in Berlin and had established himself in that field of business over a few years.

I had been introduced to him by another Albanian, Artim Sakiri.

In April 2000, North Macedonia played Albania in a friendly out in Prilep and Artim played for the home nation.

Despite his Albanian heritage, he also qualified to play for the North Macedonians who won the match 1-0.

Artim earned his living with another Bundesliga 2 side, Tennis Borussia Berlin, and although we were opponents in the international match, we travelled back to Germany together from Skopje.

He had mentioned Fali to me and upon his introduction, the agent and I became quite friendly.

However, it was not directly through these two friends that I was able to move on to another club although they were both looking out for me.

That occurred through the hospitality of another Albanian friend, Xhelil Musa, who owned a hotel in Hamburg.

As an exiled Albanian, Xhelil had watched on with growing horror and bewilderment at the country of his birth as it went through that civil war period of 1997–98.

I have already spoken about the lawlessness, the guns, the corruption and a government struggling against the tide to implement curfews and rules.

It was in the spirit of sportsmanship that Xhelil reached out to Astrit Hafizi and offered accommodation for the national team as we prepared for that vital game against Germany out in Hannover.

Over a 10 to 12-day period, he looked after us as we focused on the game ahead and, as captain of the team, I had established a working relationship and friendship with this Albanian hotel owner.

In the pre-season of 2002, Astrit Hafizi, in his capacity as sporting director of my former club, Vllaznia Shkoder, had approached Xhelil about his squad coming out to Hamburg to kick-start their sessions for the upcoming campaign.

Astrit knew that I was out of contract, and he offered me training facilities with Vllaznia while they were in the German city. At that time, Annfrances was coming close to her due date and so we decided that she should return home to be with her mum and dad while I trained with Vllaznia and tried to get a club.

I worked through the sessions with the team, but, determined to be with Annfrances for the birth of our child, I returned home in late July, narrowly missing out on that birth by a couple of hours!

Our first son Ruan was born on the 25th of the month.

The name, incidentally, is a direct and deliberate amalgamation of the first two letters of our names. Ru for Rudi – An for Annfrances.

And so, now I was ready to embrace one of life's greatest responsibilities – parenthood.

At such times, one must weigh things up.

I needed to make a decision now, and not just for two people – now I was making a decision for my family.

It is a heavy responsibility and I thought of the great sacrifices that both my parents had made for myself and my brother Aleks as we were growing up in Albania.

Ruan's early life would differ greatly from mine. He would never have to come to terms with oppression and tyranny. Never have to look over his shoulder and watch what he was saying in case it brought trouble to his door from anonymous whispers.

He would grow up from a free-born child to a free-born man, but his mother and I would instil in him our values of family life, sharing and sacrifice that we had learned from our own parents.

In time, we would also pass that on to his younger brother, Rocco, who was yet to come.

For the moment though, my first priority was to provide for my family and a possible route to that was to go back to my past and where it had all begun for me at Vllaznia Shkoder.

When I had made my debut for my hometown club back then, I lined up with the experienced defender Hysen Dedja, another Shkoder native like me, who, incidentally, also happened to be the brother-in-law of Astrit Hafizi.

In 2002, he was the manager of Vllaznia and he wanted me to come back to the club and I, of course, was tempted. Hysen knew me as a person of good character and, I suppose, my experience in playing in three different countries as well as my international caps, were an incentive to take me to the club.

However, the deal was not a good one financially and, as I have said, I needed to think about my family now, in terms of security.

It was at that point that I heard from the man who had been the prime minister of the country and who would go on to be president, Illir Meta.

Nowadays, he is fondly feted as being a big Celtic supporter and, he it was, who was president and founder of the Celtic Supporters' Club of Albania.

In 2002, he had just stepped down as prime minister, but he was involved in some capacity with KF Tirana, the most successful club in the country and he spoke to the chairman, an Egyptian named Metwally El Sayed, about the possibility of me coming to the club.

Meta called me and told me that El Sayed wanted me and that he would be offering me a deal.

And, what a deal!

It was more than I was earning in the Bundesliga 2 and he was throwing in an apartment as well for me and my family to live in.

To be honest, the offer was four times more than I was being presented with at Vllaznia, so it was a case of the head ruling over the heart.

On sentimental grounds, it would have been nice to go back to my hometown team where it had all started for me, but realistically, it was impossible to turn down the money at KF Tirana.

The signing-on fee looked attractive as well, although there would be a story about that, further down the line.

I was 33 years of age, and I was starting to listen to my body – beginning to understand that I did not have too many more seasons left in the game.

I knew my body was different from the Rudi Vata of even five years before and so I started to prepare for the end of the journey.

My reactions were different, and I had to analyse that in a completely different way.

So, there I was, 11 years on from that moment when I had left my homeland in search of a better life, a better world and now I was back where it all began for me in professional football – the capital of Albania, Tirana.

I felt it was important for me to go back and the environment, on the surface, was a good one and yet so much had changed.

I suppose it was understandable for a people who had never really had anything to suddenly become consumed by materialism.

In that post-civil unrest period, corruption was rife.

In my view, the politicians were all corrupt, out for their own selves and not really interested in developing the country.

I am not entirely sure that my opinion of that has changed, even now. Was this the Albania that I had longed for all those years before?

Was this the country that was the best place to take my family and raise my son? It was hard to tell.

On the football front, I found the transition comparatively easy. The standard of the top league was low and not what I was used to with Celtic, Apollon or Cottbus.

KF Tirana were coasting it domestically, but we went out of the UEFA Cup to the Romanians, National Bucharest.

I found that I could easily adapt to the demands of the game in Tirana and, it has to be said, I was earning a wage that I could never have dreamt possible back when I was a young man growing up in the country.

I thought back to the early days at Dinamo when one had to use initiative in order to make some money.

Back when I in my late teens and early 20s, you could spot the professional footballers in the country. They had a uniform quite unlike anything else that was available to the ordinary working Albanians.

Levi's jeans.

Calvin Klein denims.

Hugo Boss dress shirts.

Benetton sweaters and cardigans.

Above all, trainers bearing the names of Adidas, Nike, Skechers and more.

They were the preserve of those who played football and, critically, did so away from home on European, Balkan or international duties. We had a word – contraband.

We were in a privileged situation in that we could go abroad and buy materials and goods that nobody else had back home.

I remember doing a brisk trade in Citizen watches.

They were a speciality, and I was able to buy currency on the black market that would let me buy the watches cheaply and sell them when I got back into the country.

Of course, it was illegal with the *Sigurimi* and you had to be careful and cunning to pull it off, but if you got it right then you could pick up, say, ten watches, bring them back into the country and sell them.

You needed to have your hiding places and I remember sewing money into the waistband of my trousers in case I got searched at the airport. Gold coins were another great source of currency. I could buy them on the black market at home and travel out of the country with them.

However, unlike the paper money, they were heavy and clunky to carry about, so I had to be clever about hiding them.

I remember coming up with a scheme that I could use on the bus to the airport. If I carried a screwdriver then I could lever open the railing above my head. This was the railing you would hold on to when standing up as you travelled. It was a perfect fit for the coins and completely undetectable.

The *Sigurimi* would be on the bus so I had to be careful about when I did this sort of thing.

The airport could present a different challenge altogether and that was passing through the metal detectors, so I devised a plan for that as well.

I got myself a source at the airport, promised him a Citizen watch, and he would take the coins from me before I went through the detectors.

Once I got to the departure gate, he would meet up with me and hand me the coins back over.

Watches, jeans, ladies' nylon scarves, sweaters and t-shirts – all of these were merchandise to me and, thanks to my football travels in those early days, I was able to build up a very successful cottage industry.

Of course, I wasn't the only one doing this, but I think I had the edge on others, probably because I was young and fearless.

Looking back, it was highly risky, but then again, wasn't everything back in pre-1992 Albania?

Equally, it made me feel good. I was striking out in my own small way, taking on the system and trying to gain those small victories and, besides, I had a network of friends who were willing to trade with me for the kind of things that people in the West took for granted.

And, as I say, I wasn't the only one doing it.

One of the most famous results ever in Albanian football was when KF Flamurtari played Barcelona at home in the 1987/88 UEFA Cup competition.

Naturally, the Catalan club were favourites for the tie but on a noteworthy night in December, in front of 18,500 supporters who squeezed into the small Flamurtari Stadium, the home side won 1-0 with a goal from famed Albanian striker Sokol Kushta in the 16th minute.

It was an amazing night and I remember it well.

This was a Barcelona side packed with international players such as Spanish goalkeeper Andoni Zubizarreta, the great German midfielder Bernd Schuster and prolific English striker, Gary Lineker. And yet, Flamurtari pulled off a shock result to take to Spain for the second leg.

However, one hour before kick-off in the famous Estadio Camp Nou, the away side were still to enter the ground. There was a simple reason for that – the squad were all out shopping!

Going to the beautiful, commercial heart of Barcelona was just too much of a temptation to buy for oneself as well as returning to Albania with some contraband to sell on.

Arguably, a shopping trip and a late arrival were not the ideal preparations for facing one of the biggest football clubs in the world on their own pitch in front of thousands of shouting Catalans.

Perhaps that's why the boys lost 3-1 on the night and went out of the tournament, but I can sympathise with their exploits.

The Albanian system of oppression meant that, when given an opportunity to make a few bucks, it was hard to resist.

We were entrepreneurs back in those days!

* * *

In the Tirana of 2002, I was finding the football less of a challenge. The intensity just wasn't there and, although I was playing for a side who were coasting towards another league title, I cannot say that I was being stretched, as the standard was poor.

Another issue was coming to the fore as well. The signing-on fee that I had expected on arrival at the club had not materialised and I felt that every time I broached the subject with Metwally El Sayed, he was deftly avoiding the situation.

Eventually, he told me that the fee would have to be postponed which, I felt, was a breaking of our agreement.

It left a bad taste in my mouth and, frankly, was souring my return to Tirana. We had an agreement. I had kept my side of the bargain and the club president appeared to be reneging on his part of the deal. I pondered my options over the Christmas of 2002, which we naturally spent in Shkoder with my parents.

That was a special time and not just because it was our first Christmas with Ruan, and we were in my hometown.

There was a priest known as Dom Simon Jubani. He came from a huge Catholic family background, entering the seminary in 1958 and, on ordination, being sent to the famous Abbey of Miredita. This was a district in the north of the country and no longer exists as it was dissolved in 2002 and replaced by a newly created county.

And then came 1963 when, for practising the Catholic religion and administering the sacraments to the people, he was arrested under the rules of the Enver Hoxha regime.

He was now to endure 26 years in Burrel Prison in a tiny cell measuring just 12 x 24 feet in size.

His brother, Dom Lazer, was himself poisoned to death, allegedly by the authorities, in 1982.

Burrel was a brutal establishment and Dom Simon's refusal to work in the punishment mines ensured that he was regularly beaten and tortured by the sadistic guards who controlled the prison.

In time, he would come to write a remarkably vivid memoir about this part of his life called *Burgjet e Mia* which translates as 'My Prisons'.

As I have written before, all religion was outlawed by Hoxha in 1967 and many of Dom Simon's fellow priests and other religious leaders were imprisoned, tortured and killed.

His survival was, in many parts, miraculous but also spoke to many Albanians about the strength of spirit and the will to endure the very worst treatment in order to be free.

Dom Simon's own freedom arrived in April 1989 when the collapsing regime released him from his captivity at long last and he could walk away from Burrel and the endless oppression and torture.

I cannot imagine what would be going through his mind at that time. Could anyone put themselves in his shoes and contemplate those 26 years of captivity and now, the mental stress that could conceivably go with his release?

We can only offer the theory, perhaps, that his faith, his belief in God, had remained resolute and a constant companion to him in those moments when he may have felt that he was descending into a hell on earth.

We do know that he retained that faith as he returned from religious and political exile to, once again, carry out his Christian and theological duties as a Roman Catholic priest.

On 11 November 1990, along with other brother priests recently released from prison, he celebrated a public Mass in a graveyard in Shkoder.

It was a huge event, and the setting could not have been more beautiful. If you ever get the opportunity to visit Shkoder, then I would strongly recommend that you seek out the funeral chapel in the graveyard grounds.

This magnificent chapel has maintained a serenity about it and is a place imbued with the kind of peace one can only get from God.

One can only speculate about how Dom Simon and his fellow concelebrants felt as they stood once again in front of their people on that cold November day and practised their religion along with administering the sacraments.

Hoxha had tried to crush the church, but you cannot crush the spirit of a people – and I was one of those people.

I attended the Mass.

I had been raised a Roman Catholic, as you know, although there was no outlet for expression of one's faith and, as I have said, I was warned by my grandmother never to utter a word about God or bless myself in public for fear of reprisals.

Annfrances is very much a practising Catholic whereas I am more passively religious. From reading this book, you will understand that I have a strong personal belief in God and his will, but I see no need to observe the rituals and strictures of organised religion.

God is all around us.

God's church is the world.

The eternal question is God – man or woman?

The earth is called 'Mother Earth' suggesting female.

The father is akin to the sun.

Together, the sun and the earth conceive of the world around us.

With light, there is energy and no darkness.

I have often discussed with local priests about not having to attend church in a dogmatic fashion when there is so much of God around us. For those who need the sacraments, I have no issue – such is their belief and comfort.

So, there I was on that November morning in 1990, attending Mass, being at one with my people and seeing clearly the changes that were taking place in my country.

It may have been one of those moments in my life when I dared to contemplate that such massive change in that country could create an opportunity for me to escape. I cannot, in all honesty, recall how I felt, but upon reflection, it is hard to see, after all these years, how it could not have affected my thinking and planted some small seed in me for the future.

Fast forward to that Christmas then, of 2002, and, in the house of my parents and a few other family members, we were in the company of Dom Simon Jubani, and he was here to baptise my son, Ruan.

We were out at my parents' house when this humble, slight man arrived in our midst. He had come at the behest of my father, Pjeter, but to my mind, he had been sent by God. He was 75 years of age and I had to marvel at how such a man could survive the life he had lived and find the strength to write a book about it.

On the day, he picked up a bucket of cold water and doused Ruan over the head whilst murmuring some prayers.

I had never been formally baptised, so this was a new experience for me to see.

And yet, despite the icy water and the sudden *splash* over Ruan, my son never once opened his eyes.

He stayed peacefully asleep.

I hoped that this was a sign that, whatever life threw at my boy, he would be able to handle it!

For the rest of us, it was a beautiful moment. A moment of full circle when I could think back to 'Uncle Ndreka' – the persecuted Catholic priest who had risked further persecution by sneaking into our house and teaching Aleks and me the Italian language.

That invaluable education had enabled me to be at one with Liam Brady when we spoke on the phone about me joining Celtic.

From a priest stealing into our house, under cover of darkness, to Dom Simon Jubani being able to stand freely in our kitchen and openly baptise the son of Rudi Vata – my country had changed a lot!

And I could not help but wonder what my parents made of it all as well. The years of secret reverence to God, never once being able to state it openly or be seen to be indulging in a life built around a faith. What a wonder this must have been to their eyes!

I enjoyed that Christmas as it brought back so many memories but also created new ones. Now we could celebrate the festive season as we had never been allowed to do when I was a child.

It was nice to be back in the land of my own people – their soil was my soil.

However, to stay on in the country meant being in an uncomfortable situation with the club and the president.

It became clear that I was not about to get the money I was owed anytime soon and, as I mentioned, the level of football was not providing enough competition for me.

And yet, it was like the summer all over again in that I might have to look for another club.

I did not realise at that time that the answer to my problem lay in the hands of one of the best footballers of his generation and a man who had remembered me from my experiences in Germany – Pierre Littbarski.

CHAPTER 17

# ASIAN ADVENTURE

In January of 2003, I was out in Egypt with KF Tirana, as we prepared for the next phase of the season in the winter break.

Given the nationality of our president, I suppose it was perfectly natural that we would be out in his country, absorbing the sun and getting the training sessions in order.

As always, I worked hard, but I still had the lingering malaise of the uncomfortable situation with Metwally El Sayed.

And then, one morning, I had a telephone call from an unrecognised number. Someone had passed my contact details on.

The Japanese League was about to get underway, and the call was from the manager of Yokohama FC.

After a very successful playing career, former German internationalist Pierre Littbarski had turned to management and was now in his second spell at Yokohama.

He had guided them to the J2 League and then, after a spell in Germany with Bayer Leverkusen as an assistant and MSV Duisburg as manager, he had returned to east Asia again.

Pierre's wife was Japanese, and he spoke the language fluently. He wanted to know if I would be interested in coming out to Tokyo and working with him.

What an opportunity! This was Pierre Littbarski, a legendary figure as a player in the German game who had been part of three World Cup Final squads, playing in one final in 1982, losing to Italy and then starting in the successful 1-0 victory over Argentina in 1990.

Such experience.

I felt I would relish working with this man and I liked the idea that he had sought me out, gone as far as to get my number, personally to ask me to come to Japan.

Now for a new challenge.

Annfrances was as keen as I was to go to Japan and we both felt it would be a great experience for Ruan as well, young as he was.

We both felt it best that I travelled out alone to get settled in before sending for them both, so I caught a flight to Rome, where I was able to pick up a travel visa, and then headed for Tokyo.

What a city.

A population of over 37 million people and yet, the streets were so clean.

I had never seen so many tall buildings in one place and, later in the year, when my father came out to visit us, all he could do was talk about the millions of lights that filled the city.

When you recall that I grew up in a Shkoder that had streetlamps, as I described in an earlier chapter, 500 yards apart and that seldom worked, you could see why my father marvelled at the brilliance of the Tokyo lighting system.

Technology was key to everything in this new country that I was in as I found out on my very first night in a Yokohama hotel.

I took a bathroom break and, without being too graphic, as I sat on the seat, contemplating my new world, I became aware of a sensation of warmth around my backside.

The toilet seats were fitted with heaters that kicked in when you sat down!

In addition, there was a jet of water that, well, you get the picture!

I thought back to my youngest days at school when we had to use the Turkish-style toilets that were common at that time.

Effectively, as I have described in an earlier chapter, the toilet was just a hole in the ground, surrounded by porcelain and the hygiene was practically zero, but it was all we knew and never questioned it.

Fast forward to me in my early 30s and I am out in Japan sitting on a state-of-the-art, heated toilet seat.

Such a contrast.

This was only part of what Japan could offer.

As to the club itself, Yokohama FC, their back story was an interesting one given that it had only been formed in the late 1990s.

It grew out of the ashes of a merger between two clubs, Yokohama Flugels and Yokohama Marinos.

Given that the clubs were city rivals, it was a bit like Celtic and Rangers merging into one club, except that they kept the original name of only one of the clubs.

Could you imagine *that* in Scotland?

One day you are the supporter of a club called Celtic and the next you are following the merged club, but they are now called Glasgow Rangers!

I think it would be safe to say that there would be a complete riot throughout Glasgow and beyond!

A group of original supporters of the Flugels viewed the merger with complete distaste, seeing it, quite simply as a dissolution of the club they had faithfully followed and so decided not to attach themselves to the new hybrid team but start a club of their own.

When they formed that club, they became the first supporter-owned professional sports team in Japan.

Even then, they were not allowed to advance to the professional league by the Japanese Football Association but were consigned to the amateur league instead, which was the third tier in the country.

Despite winning the title in their first season, they were still not allowed to move up to the second tier until winning the title again the following season.

Pierre Littbarski had been a bold appointment by the club, but consecutive league titles ensured that it was an excellent move.

Yokohama would offer me experiences that I could never have dreamed of back in my younger days.

The environment was very relaxed, as were the people.

Throughout my football career, I had played in front of hugely divided crowds.

The Glasgow derby between Celtic and Rangers was imbued with a hatred cut across, in my opinion, by ridiculous religious division and that 90-minute animosity could be thoroughly unpleasant even if, out on the pitch, you were able to shut it out and concentrate on your game. Seriously – one of the biggest matches in the world, but I often wondered if that world could see the hate when they tuned in on television.

Cyprus had its fair share of partisan rivalry between supporters, although not religious and, in the big derby games, it was not unusual to see flares going off and one section of fans hollering abuse at the other.

I have already detailed that game from my first season for Dinamo Tirana that concluded with a riot and our team bus becoming a burnt-out shell as arsonists set fire to it.

Even in Germany, a lot of clubs had their 'ultras' – that self-proclaimed group who professed loyalty to the team but had that undercurrent of intimidation among their swollen ranks.

Japan?

Japan was entirely different. The self-effacement and deference from both sets of supporters was refreshing if a little difficult to comprehend at first.

I discovered that win, lose, or draw, the outcome was always the same. The supporters would stand and applaud the team as they left the pitch almost as if they were thanking you for the spectacle and your efforts – which, I suppose, they were in a way.

It was not unusual for fans to turn up at training sessions with presents for the team and I got quite used to being presented with an envelope containing photographs from our recent matches, whether we had had a favourable result or not. They photographed everything!

Unfailingly polite, grateful and respectful of you and the job you did for the team – that could sum up the typical Japanese football supporter.

Indeed, I would say that, as a people, they exuded a serenity and quiet peace that I certainly had never before encountered. It was refreshing.

I had arrived at an interesting moment in Japanese sporting history.

There was a sea change under way.

For many years, the national sport was the famous sumo wrestling with professional baseball, as an American import, also a hugely popular choice for enthusiasts.

However, I came to the country after one of the biggest sporting events on the planet had taken place – the World Cup.

The political machinations involved to settle on the first ever joint-staging of the tournament in history between South Korea and Japan would become a matter of record, but if the primary intention of the founders of the World Cup was to create a festival to spread the global appeal of the game into hitherto unknown football oases, then Asia was a good choice.

The tournament had been a critical success and both the Japanese and South Korean public had bought into the spirit of the occasion with great crowds at all the matches plus television viewing figures in the millions.

Perhaps the seeds of such modern Japanese players as Kyogo Furuhashi, Tomoki Iwata and Daizen Maeda following in the footsteps of the brilliantly gifted Shunsuke Nakamura by coming to Celtic, were sown around this time. Who can say? All I know is that there was a surge of interest in the game as I arrived in the country.

Pierre Littbarski was an intelligent guy who had new ideas about how the game should be played and the fact that he was able to speak to a lot of his squad in their native language was a factor in the success that he had previously enjoyed.

He was great to work with and had a novel way of rewarding you if you were nominated as the Man of the Match. It was not uncommon to receive a brand-new Sony phone or camera to mark the occasion.

I was one of four foreign players at the club including Dutch defender Mathieu Boots, veteran Argentine centre-back Fernando Morner and a name perhaps familiar to British football supporters, German forward Dirk Lehmann, who played for Fulham, Hibernian, Brighton & Hove Albion and Motherwell. Dirk, who also played for Energie Cottbus in the season before I had gone to Germany, was another who had arrived in Japan at the same time as myself.

The rest of my team-mates were Japanese nationals of whom, perhaps, striker Shoji Jo was the most recognisable as he had played most of his career in the country with a detour to Spain for a year with Real Valladolid into the bargain.

A Japanese international, he developed a knee injury out in Spain that curtailed his involvement, so he returned to Japan and came to Yokohama in 2003 as well.

He was our top scorer in that season, but it was a tough one for the club as we finished 11th out of 12 in the J2 League.

I was able to contribute in about half of our domestic fixtures and was possibly feeling the effects of my energy draining away.

Ruan was learning to walk, and he was a very active child so instead of going back to relax after a hard training session, I would return home and Annfrances and I would take him out to the big parks that were plentiful both in Yokohama and Tokyo.

The parks gave us a chance to breathe good air and the city also gave us the opportunity to visit Tokyo Disneyland, so, as a family, we were experiencing different things.

I knew, in my heart, that my playing career was coming to a conclusion, but my life balance was in a really good place.

Yes, being a man of family and a new father meant that, for the first time in my life, I did not have to focus solely on football but on other aspects of my life to achieve happiness.

Yokohama looked after us brilliantly and in a very honest way.

Honesty.

I afford that word huge respect. The game of football is too important, too precious to allow dishonesty in it. I despise those who seek to fix matches, to cheat and scam not just the players out on the park but the supporters as well.

These are the fans who go to the matches or gather around television sets to buy into the sport, and they deserve the cleanest contest that they can see.

In many ways, I have made sacrifices in my life to play this game and the last thing I want to see is those who seek to take advantage of others to exploit and corrupt sport and fair competition.

In Japan, I saw an integrity and honesty around the game. The World Cup was changing things and people were turning more and more to football as an outlet for their sporting instinct.

Yokohama were looking after the game as well as my family and others who bought into the institution.

The club paid for our apartment, furnished us with cars and even arranged a private sponsorship deal for me from main club sponsors, Hummel.

We had no complaints.

The apartment was on the seventh floor, so the views were magnificent.

In saying that, there was a day when I was giving Ruan a wash over the bath. I think Annfrances was in the kitchen preparing some food.

It was late September.

The bath was very small as they tend to be in the country, and I was leaning over it with my boy cradled in my left arm. My right hand was scooping up the water with a sponge and wiping down Ruan's body.

Suddenly, there was a huge rumble, the building started to sway, and Ruan slipped away from my arm straight into the bath – earthquake! I picked him up quickly, slid across the floor and shouted to Annfrances to take cover.

My experiences in both Albania and Cyprus meant that I was not unused to a tremor, and I knew what I had to do – sit in the doorframe where the support is above your head.

I positioned myself there, holding tightly on to Ruan as I did so.

Any earthquake I had ever experienced was for about 15 to 20 seconds, but right here in Japan, this one seemed to go on for two minutes! As you can imagine, the longest two minutes ever!

From where I was sitting, I could feel the sway of the building and then, hear its metal frame starting to creak ominously.

I knew that the Japanese had designed and built their high-rises to withstand a fairly extensive reading on the Richter scale, but in those moments, when I could hear the grinding of the metal, the groan of the building, I could not be sure how much the building could take!

What a terrifying sound and, it has to be said, one that I will never forget. For two whole minutes, we were powerless and, in a sense, trapped. I knew that you could not get in a lift and even to attempt to evacuate the building by going down the emergency stairs would have been as foolish as it was potentially life-threatening.

We had to sit, ride it out and hope that God was on our side.

Eventually, it stopped, although I knew, from previous experience, that the aftershocks could last for days.

I had to marvel at the ingenuity of Japanese architecture, design and builders that could make such a tall edifice withstand the strain of what later was named the Tokachi-Oko earthquake.

When you consider that the epicentre of the quake was in the island of Hokkaido, some 1,300 kilometres from the capital city, it gives you some idea of its overall power.

The power of nature.

A reminder that you are always at the mercy of it.

Japan is a beautiful country – a massive country with exceptional people.

You got the feeling that there was no obvious crime on the streets of Tokyo, such was the safety you felt when taking your family around the place.

In addition, facilities were among the best I have ever experienced in a country.

We ate out a lot as a family as this seemed to be established practice in Tokyo.

Perhaps people worked so hard that it was difficult to find the time to cook or, maybe, the simple notion of going out to a restaurant brought a family together. Let someone else cook for you and relax with your friends and family as you talk about your day, your life.

It was certainly a lifestyle that we enjoyed.

Of course, it was a huge challenge to come to such a distant country and earn a living, but I have already established in this book, I hope, that I enjoyed travelling – enjoyed the experiences of new countries, new walks of life.

Never in my imagination as a child could I have envisaged that, one day, I would live and work in such a place as Japan.

Once again, football, the beautiful game, had presented these opportunities to me and my family.

Bringing my father to Tokyo would have been completely unthinkable to me as a young man starting off in the game and yet, here we were, my father's eyes and mind taking in the sensations of a city like Tokyo with its 24-hour pace and, as he constantly mentioned, the endless, bright streetlights.

It took me back to the marvels of Amsterdam again as I, as a member of the Albanian under-18s squad, wandered around those streets enthralled by the lights, the sounds and the peace.

The West had opened up to me as a young man and now, the East had as well, and I was always excited and hungry for new life challenges.

It pleased me that I was not a 'no-man' who was afraid to take up new responsibilities. When faced by such responsibilities, such tests of my courage and resolve, I would always look to the positive – always be a guy that would say *yes* to new opportunities, new challenges.

It was a mantra that had served me well.

I was at an age and a stage of my life where I could appreciate all that was around me and all that I had achieved from playing the game.

From Shkoder to Tirana, Paris, Glasgow, Paradise, Germany, Japan and beyond.

My contract at Yokohama was winding down and, at the end of 2003, having thoroughly enjoyed almost a year of the Japanese lifestyle, learning from it and exposing my family to the benefits of it, I was now having to think about the potential end game of my playing career.

## CHAPTER 18

# END GAMES – NEW BEGINNINGS

We returned as a family to Scotland for Christmas in 2003.

Ruan was around a year and a half old, and we thought it would be good for Annfrances and her family to have Christmas together for a change.

Aleks was also in Scotland, and I was looking forward to catching up with him as well.

In the meantime, with the conclusion of my contract with Yokohama, I was turning my attention to going to another football club.

I had been in talks with a couple more Japanese sides and there was interest from Cyprus again, but one day, I had a call from a Scottish football agent named Raymond Sparkes.

Raymond was one of the big players in the agency industry with contacts throughout the country and he told me that, having had a conversation with St Johnstone manager, Billy Stark, that my one-time assistant manager at Celtic would like to take me to Perth until the end of the current season.

At that point, St Johnstone were in the Scottish First Division, which was the second-tier league in the country, having been relegated two seasons before after five years in the top flight.

They were battling to get promoted and Billy was looking to bring some experience to his squad.

They had some good players in their ranks with Finnish internationalist Mixu Paatelainen having joined in the summer.

Mixu had around 70 caps for his country and his professional career had taken him to Dundee United, Aberdeen, Bolton Wanderers, Wolverhampton Wanderers, Hibernian and more. Wherever he went, he scored goals and, indeed, would end up as top scorer for us in that season of 2003/04.

In addition, a couple of boys who were coming through the squads when I was at Celtic, Simon Donnelly and Chris Hay, were also on St Johnstone's books.

Then there was Jim Weir, Peter McDonald and Mark Reilly – guys who had also been around the Scottish scene for a while.

The overtures that were made to me started off as an invitation to come in and train with the first team and see if we could develop something from there, so I did.

It seemed like a good environment to work in and the travelling to Perth and back was not exactly a hardship.

In addition, maybe it was time for us, as a family, to settle a wee bit longer back in Scotland.

I was willing to sign up for the club but that's when the red tape took over.

Despite the fact that I had what I considered to be an exceptionally clean record of financial health, a bought and paid-for property in Scotland, and a son born in the country, I *still* had to go through the visa system for a work permit.

I had to go back out to Albania and apply for it in person.

Although I have never conceived of myself being of less value than any British person, I have always felt that the UK government had a way of treating me and, probably my fellow Albanians, as second- or third-class citizens.

I feel that they still do in many respects.

I had spent my life and my career building a reputation for myself so that I could enjoy a place in society.

You do not get to live comfortably in Germany, for example, without proving yourself to the Germans. Living with them, working among them and representing yourself in the best possible way so that you can earn that respect.

I would certainly say the same of the Japanese.

In every country in which I have worked, I have strived to be the best person that I can be.

Rudi works hard.

Rudi pays his way.

Rudi is reliable.

Rudi is valued.

My reputation is important to me. In the final analysis, one's reputation is everything.

Eventually, I was given clearance by the authorities to play for St Johnstone and I made my debut in a 3-0 defeat to Motherwell in the Scottish Cup.

The national cup competition was important, of course, but the real deal for Billy Stark and the St Johnstone support was to gain promotion back to the big time and the Scottish Premier Division. I must admit, I was disappointed with the standard in the Scottish game when I came back to the country. Football did not seem to have changed since my days at Celtic.

In the eight years since I had played in the country, I had had an education in new approaches to the game, the best of which, I have said already, was my time in Germany.

Cyprus and Japan also had their own variations and coaches who valued work ethic, stamina, speed, movement and above all, discipline.

However, to me, Germany should be the benchmark for the game with their *all-in* approach to methods and training.

It has not changed in all these years, from what I have seen.

Listen, I was now playing in the second tier of Scottish football, so I could not have expected the pedigree of the likes of Bayern Munich or Borussia Dortmund, but there did not seem to be any new ideas on display.

I liked Billy Stark. He was a gentleman in the way he conducted himself and I really wanted to do a job for him.

He, in my opinion, was more of a thinker: a calm individual who was not given to histrionics on the touchline but kept an innate peace with himself. When it was time to impart what he wanted out on the park, he would soon let us know about it, but perhaps he was up against it and sometimes supporters like to see that bit of passion coming from the dugout.

A manager who shouts and gesticulates for 90 minutes, but that was not Billy's style.

We were battling through the season and there was no clear favourite for the title. Clyde ran a close second to Inverness Caledonian Thistle at the end of the campaign and we finished a fairly distant third.

We had the beating of both Inverness and Clyde on a couple of occasions, but ultimately, too many drawn games and the dropped points incurred holed us beneath our waterline.

There was one infamous game that I can recall against Raith Rovers at their ground, Starks Park, in Kirkcaldy. With about six fixtures left to play and the chance to close the gap at the top of the table with Clyde, we ended up relying on a Simon Donnelly penalty to get us a 1-1 draw.

Another level finish that could have blown the title race open a bit more had we managed to secure a win and the three points.

However, the reason I will never forget this match is the injury I sustained, from a 'tackle', in the first half.

Rovers, at that time, had Spanish attacking midfielder Antonio Calderon as their player-coach at the club.

Calderon had spent the vast majority of his career in his native Spain, most notably with Rayo Vallecano and Lleida, but he was now seeing out his career in Scottish football.

According to the report in the following day's *Sunday Mail* newspaper, the Spaniard and I *clashed* just before half-time.

*CLASHED?*

As far as I was concerned, it was a brutal assault. Calderon raked the studs of his boot across my head as I challenged him.

I was left with a black eye, a cut nose and a head wound gushing blood that required three stitches when I got back to the dressing room.

And Calderon was not even booked for the challenge!

I could not believe that and told the press so after the game.

Better than that, I made sure Calderon knew about it when we resumed hostilities after the break.

I tell you what, he bloody *knew* that he had got away with one on me, but as I said to the press after the match, no one likes to admit that they are wrong.

At half-time, the doctor asked me if I wanted to return to the pitch. There was never any question about that, but I was feeling quite dizzy and, I suppose, in today's climate, a player would never be allowed to go back into action with a head injury like that.

Missing out on promotion was a severe blow for the club, of course and, ultimately, Billy Stark paid for it with his job.

In complete honesty, I did not really enjoy my stay at St Johnstone.

Perhaps it was the situation the club found itself in financially as they appeared to have gambled a bit on a quick return to the Premier Division.

A lot of clubs in similar situations do that as they pay over the market value for players, management et cetera, and hope that bouncing back up will be compensated for when you get big gates regularly the following year against Celtic, Rangers, Hibernian, Hearts, Aberdeen and the rest.

It is a risky strategy, but I did sense there was a tension around McDiarmid Park based on the pressure of getting back up. It was easy to see.

But I felt it was even more than that. There was a lack of atmosphere which made me feel the club was dead and I concluded that there was no energy coming from the fans.

That flatness contributed to a deficit of energy around the place and when the energy levels drop, in my opinion, that very often leads to negativity and negative results.

Equally, to my mind, a winning mentality was not totally evident in the players.

I cannot stress enough how important that is in any sport.

Instilling an inherent belief in your ability to overcome the odds and dig out a winning performance is critical in those moments when the margins between defeat and victory are narrow.

We were too passive in that season and ultimately, that cost us dear.

Such, I felt, was the case with St Johnstone during my short spell up in Perth. I was now approaching the end of my football career. At 35, I had travelled the world to fulfil my ambitions and as I headed into the close season, I wondered where my next port of call could be, if at all.

That summer, we headed to Cannes in France for a holiday and a chance to recharge my energy levels.

Over that two-week period, I had some agents calling me from various outposts.

I heard there was interest coming from St Mirren who, at that point, were, like St Johnstone, in the second tier of Scottish football.

Again, there were some overtures from Japan but nothing particularly concrete and I was also having talks with Partizani Tirana.

I came to terms with the fact that I was not necessarily enjoying my football.

That awakening in the morning when I would consciously look forward to the game, the match, the contest, was beginning to gradually drift away from me.

My body, the body that I had worked away on for years to achieve a tough physicality, was feeling the effects of the professional game.

I suppose that happens to all athletes.

Cannes was beautiful and hot. The holiday was fantastic, but just like any other time that I was away during the summer, I would train.

And I was hammering myself.

Long runs in high temperatures – plenty of sit-ups and swimming – cardiovascular work.

Throughout my career, I had prided myself on my fitness and I was not about to let that drop.

I felt fit, healthy, strong – and, yet …

… and, yet. Something was happening to me. It was organic, natural, unavoidable.

My head was talking to me.

My body was talking to me.

And they were both saying … *Rudi; it is time. It is time.*

Rudi Vata had always trusted his instincts.

They had taken me from the austerity of communist Albania to the prosperity of western Europe and eastern Asia with so many learning experiences along the way.

I had been blessed in my playing career and now, as I contemplated the conclusion of that journey, I arrived at a peaceful agreement with myself.

It was time.

Of course, my emotions were mixed.

I had been a professional athlete from the age of 18. I had dedicated myself to football – made the sacrifices required to attain my goals.

From that boy who had smacked a ball off a wall in his bare feet, on the soil streets of Shkoder to the man who had captained his country – I had given it my all because the game brings its own rewards, both financial and spiritual.

Was I sad? Yes, of course.

The ending of anything is always imbued with some form of sadness.

It lies in wait for you to ambush those moments of contentedness, but I could see through that and wanted to take my path forward.

Annfrances announced to me that she was pregnant and that we could look forward to our second child in the spring of 2005 and so, I thought, *I am to become a father again*.

And so, I made the decision. It *was* time, Rudi. It *was* time.

* * *

And yet, it is never an easy decision, I believe, for any sportsman to call time on their playing career.

An athlete invests so much to take themselves to the highest level.

Sacrifice. Such a key word.

What are *you* prepared to do to make it?

What are *you* prepared to sacrifice?

When it comes to that moment when you have to decide about your approach to your sport and career – what decision do you make?

I have seen it so many times in my football life. The players I played with and against had varying degrees of attitude.

Some dedicated themselves to their craft, shaping their entire commitment based on discipline, hard work and self-sacrifice.

Others drifted through the game, perhaps naturally talented, focusing on outside pursuits to the detriment, I think, of their careers.

With Rudi Vata, there was no other way.

I am on record as saying that I knew that I would not be the greatest player in the world but that I would always be hard to beat on application and work rate.

I believed that I had delivered on those factors throughout my life as a professional football player and now there was a bridge to cross.

A bridge that all footballers must cross.

It's that one that takes you from active player to former player.

In my time, I have seen how that can affect some of my fellow pros.

Some flourish and some struggle, sometimes slipping into a downward spiral of depression and, in a way, I can understand that.

Effectively, as a professional football player, you can get hooked on the adrenaline of the 90 minutes. The adulation.

The fans chanting your name.

Those moments when you score a goal and run to the crowd as they have this mass orgy of excitement, release and utter joy.

It is a drug and, just like any other drug, when one must wean oneself off it, that can present a problem.

I was determined that this would not happen to me.

Certainly, with the impending birth of my second child, I had a focus.

This time it would be different.

This time, I would be there for the birth, which I was, on 18 April 2005 when, not only was I present, but I also cut the umbilical cord and welcomed my second son, Rocco, to the world.

However, during the gestation of Annfrances' pregnancy, I had to focus on my next move.

Football had been good to me, and we were on a strong financial footing, so there was no direct need to rush headlong into something for the sake of the money.

However, I had been germinating a seed for some while.

My time in the game and, it must be said, my travels around the world to kick a football, had given me that priceless commodity in business – contacts.

Now was the time to use those contacts.

I felt that I could do a good job as a football agent. After all, I had been involved many transfers and many deals throughout my playing career.

I had seen the benefits of having a skilled negotiator in the room when it came to dealing with clubs and, in particular, the directors of clubs.

My profile was good, and I was fluent in a few languages, both of which I saw as assets.

The route into football agency meant that I would have to attain a badge from the Albanian Football Federation that would give me credibility around the clubs.

It would be an official FIFA licence but had to be issued to me out of Albania, because I would be travelling under that passport, so I made an appointment in Tirana to do the course.

Having worked in the game for so many years, I found the course and subsequent test to qualify for the badge quite straightforward.

You had to study the business of transfers, learn about training compensations, and understand the legalities involved in moving players from one club to another or, as was very often the case, one country to another.

The test took about an hour to complete and at the end of it I was now Rudi Vata – football agent.

No longer would I be under contract at a club.

I was the owner of myself, which was my ultimate ambition.

There was a fee, of course, and back then, it was around 1,000 Euros.

I had to put up a guarantee of 250,000 Swiss Francs, which was akin to a deposit, almost like an insurance system.

There was always the danger that a deal could go down as a bad move, and you had to protect yourself and your player in the event of that happening.

I now had to learn my craft by participation, so I started to look around at the young talent available in Albania as that appeared to be the natural choice.

Sometimes the best way to initiate a deal would be to contact a club and ask them the profile of what they were looking for in a player.

Goalkeeper? Defender? Forward? Midfielder?

What age bracket?

Were they looking for experience, a finished article or a youth to develop?

And crucially – what is your budget?

The budget was everything. Every player has his price.

Once these issues were identified then I could liaise with other agents, the many contacts I had made in the game or just friends who could perhaps help out.

It was a networking process, of course.

I had a call from my parents one day as they said there had been an article written about the fact that I was now the first former Albanian footballer to become an agent.

They told me they were getting besieged by people knocking on their door at all times of the day and night asking if I could get a move for their young sons who were playing in Shkoder.

This is what happens when the media get involved in your life.

For my part, a lot of my friends from my playing days had moved into management in countries such as Romania, Bulgaria, Hungary, Switzerland, Germany and more, so I had plenty of scope to operate within as I set about the task.

I had initial success moving some young Albanian talent into these countries, especially Bulgaria.

My focus was on their development. You cannot just trade a young player into another country, another culture and leave them to it.

You must be involved. Make sure they are well looked after and able to develop to their full potential, whatever that may be.

In those early days, I had a lot of energy for the process, and I enjoyed the challenge. Travelling was never a worry to me although I did want to be at home for my family.

I was learning fast and seeing the game from the other side.

When you play then your focus is primarily on preparation. Everything that you do, fitness, training, tactical, dietary, mental attitude – all of that is focused on the next game.

In a sense, you shut out the rest of the world and that is how it should be, because everything you achieve in the game will come down to your performances and so, just like a formula one racing car, you need to maintain the highest standards in order to compete.

When you move out of that world and into the world of business, your focus is different, although I always felt that the attributes I had as a player – mindset, character, personality – were transferable assets to my new role.

I also learned that the bigger the deal, the bigger the sharks!

Oh yes, they were there.

Maybe I was a bit too naïve about that – a bit too honest.

I wanted to look a player in the eyes and tell him the truth.

If there was an interested club, I would tell him.

When you have the sharks, very often people who had not played the game, then they would tell a player they had about

15 different clubs looking at him, even when that was not the case.

It is a failing, I still feel, in footballers that they prefer the lie.

So much easier to flatter a young player and build up that ego, but I strongly felt that path of lies was the wrong way to go about the business and their career.

In many ways, I believed I was right.

As I said, the early days were exciting, and I had the energy but there were times when that energy could get sapped.

CHAPTER 19

# THE BITTER TASTE

One of the most high-profile deals I was involved with came around in 2006.

At the time, Tony Mowbray was manager of Hibernian Football Club, and he was moulding an excellent, young and energetic side in the Scottish Premiership.

They had some real up-and-coming talent in their ranks.

Alongside defenders Steven Whittaker and Gary Caldwell, they had Kevin Thomson and Scott Brown in midfield, all four of whom would go on to represent their country at international level.

Up front, Mowbray had a pair of jewels named Derek Riordan and Garry O'Connor.

I was approached by a Serbian friend of mine who was working for Russian Premier League club Lokomotiv Moscow to say that they were looking for high-profile strikers.

Having watched both players closely, I recommended either one of Riordan and O'Connor or both.

Lokomotiv manager Slavoljub Muslin was interested so I made contact with the Hibernian chairman at the time, Rod Petrie, to see if he was open to discussing the situation.

Muslin, as a Serbian, was the first foreign manager of the club, which brought a different type of pressure, but he had enjoyed a successful career as a player and a manager, so he could handle himself.

The club's star man was Dmitri Sychev, a Russian native who had joined the club at the start of 2004 and, in a season when Lokomotiv won the title, he was named the Russian Player of the Year.

He was a pacy player who could assist and score goals at the same time and, consequently, he was dubbed the 'Russian Michael Owen' by the press after the English striker who had a high profile around the world.

His success continued with the capture of the Russian Super Cup but in the early part of August 2005, he sustained an anterior cruciate ligament injury which ruled him out for the majority of the season.

This was why, by the early part of 2006, Lokomotiv Moscow were in the market for a striker.

Derek Riordan had been a rising star at Hibernian, being voted the PFA Young Player of the Year and the Scottish Football Writers' Player of the Year in 2005, but at the end of that season, he had put in a transfer request.

Hibernian had accepted, in principle, a bid of £500,000 from Cardiff City, but Riordan did not want to move to Wales and by the early part of 2006, the situation remained unresolved.

Having spoken to Petrie, I was told that Riordan was not remotely interested in going to Russia to play his football and had turned any talks on the subject down flat.

I was a little surprised that I did not get the chance to discuss it with him. The salary was to be a lucrative one and, although I could appreciate that the change of culture would be a mammoth one and that if he was not willing to stay in the United Kingdom with a Welsh club like Cardiff, then a move out to Russia would seem even more remote, I believed the chance to earn a top salary would, at least, initiate a chat.

I was wrong on that front which, as I say, was a little surprising.

Celtic and Rangers entered the frame for him, and Riordan would go on to sign for my old club under manager Gordon Strachan in the pre-season of 2006/07.

However, I was told by Petrie that Gary O'Connor *was* interested in the move.

His agent at the time was the former Hearts and Scotland midfielder, Gary Mackay.

Gary's playing career at the Edinburgh club had been a distinguished one and I still believe he holds the record for the most competitive appearances of any Hearts player so, he was a well-known face on the Scottish scene.

He had been doing agency work for a few years but had no experience of the Russian market, so I helped to facilitate a deal.

Garry O'Connor signed for Lokomotiv Moscow in March 2006. He would be on a wage that would substantially outweigh the one he had at Hibernian by an estimated ten times and, given that Hibernian received their record sum at the time of £2.5 million and that Gary Mackay would get his agency fee, I felt that everybody was happy with the arrangement.

To his credit, Garry O'Connor donated his portion of the transfer fee back to Hibernian so that they could develop a training ground, which I felt was a magnificent gesture on his part.

I had done my job, picked up a consideration for my part in the facilitation of the deal, and was content to move on.

On the surface, Garry was having a successful initial transition to Lokomotiv Moscow.

He formed a good partnership with Dmitri Sychev and appeared to be well-liked by the home support.

His greatest moment, I would suggest, was in May 2007 when he came on as a substitute in the Russian Cup Final against great city rivals FC Moscow and scored an extra-time winner in his side's 1-0 victory.

I was in the crowd that day, alongside Scottish international assistant manager, Andy Watson, and the pair of us watched on as Garry lifted the trophy.

Watson had been sent out by the new Scotland manager, Alex McLeish, to get a look at Garry and see how he was performing with a view to recalling him to the international scene.

Interestingly, Slavoljub Muslin had been replaced as manager in October 2006 after an indifferent start to the season and a UEFA Cup exit to Belgian side, SV Zulte Waregem.

When Garry scored that winner, the man in charge at the time was respected former Russian international striker Anatoly Byshovets but even the cup win was not enough to save *his* job.

Such managerial uncertainty in the boardroom suggested that the club was in turmoil – as was Garry O'Connor.

However, I was surprised when he contacted me directly at the end of that season.

He told me that he had broken his contract with Gary Mackay, had struggled with settling in due to family circumstances and wanted to leave Russia.

Could I help him?

I went and spoke to his family and his girlfriend.

Garry was on a high salary, living in a million-dollar apartment in the centre of Moscow complete with chandeliers, which, if I recall, belonged to a Russian politician, but he was, quite simply, homesick.

He missed his girlfriend and, more crucially, his baby boy.

I had to feel for him.

It's a matter of record that Garry has had his personal and health problems and living on his own in a foreign city, especially one that could be as intimidating as Moscow, was taking its toll on him.

The cup final goal was viewed as a redemption of sorts for him, as he had been in and out of the team that season, but he put that down to family reasons and an inability to settle in the Russian capital.

Being all alone, unable to speak the language and in inconsistent form were all conspiring to affect him.

The positive was that, at only 24, he still had a potentially promising career ahead of him.

I had heard through sources that Birmingham City, under former Norwich City and Manchester United defender Steve Bruce, were very interested in bringing Garry to the Midlands.

Steve was a guy I respected.

I had played against him and United in 1995 for Paul McStay's testimonial match at Celtic Park.

We had won 3-1 in what was, effectively a friendly, albeit the legend was that Manchester United and Celtic never play friendlies!

That was an emotional night for Paul, club captain as well as my friend, and you could feel the love that poured around the ground for him as he strolled about the pitch at full time with his wife and young family in close attendance.

I had swapped jerseys with Steve that night and felt we had a connection.

I think that Gary Mackay was reluctant to deal with the Russians, and that this may have been why Garry O'Connor cancelled their contract and asked me to intervene.

There were so many clubs interested in him, but Birmingham City were first up to propose a deal.

Thus began an interesting and, I have to say, ultimately distasteful period in my agency career.

In the first instance, I had to go to Russia, on my own.

This was quite an undertaking.

If you have never been to Moscow, then I would certainly recommend it.

The Russian capital is a beautiful and interesting place to go to, but you need to be careful.

Through my connections, I knew how it could be.

The city is served by more than a few terminals and I landed at Sheremetyevo Alexander S. Pushkin Airport, which is about 30 kilometres from the centre of Moscow.

This was an area heavily populated by Chechens and the Second Chechen War between the forces of Russia and Chechnya was still ongoing, so tensions were high.

Anyone from outside the country was viewed with suspicion and stories remained about foreign visitors who had landed here, been spotted with their luggage by certain taxi drivers, got into an unmarked car and never saw the sunlight again!

What you notice about the police, officials, the military is what I call a *fear factor*.

It was a constant presence throughout my time out in Moscow, a vast sprawling city in which one can easily get lost – or worse.

Everywhere you go, you are viewed with suspicion.

You are from the West, and, in some cases, that can be spotted a mile away.

I had to adopt a persona – an Albanian persona.

It was important that I stood up to this and imposed myself on the day-to-day stuff as well as impending negotiations.

I am Rudi Vata.

I am an Albanian.

You cannot intimidate me, and I showed that to the taxi driver who picked me up at the airport.

He sported a scar on the side of his cheek and exuded a determined menace about him, but I fashioned a hard expression on my face and remained resolute.

One sign of weakness – one moment when you looked out of your depth, could be instrumental in your downfall.

I am not stupid. I knew that there could be trouble, but I remained calm and in control of myself.

When Garry spoke to Scotland manager, Alex McLeish about me, Alex told him that he had got the right guy to do the job.

Alex felt that Garry required discipline and guidance, both of which he knew I could provide.

Equally, I was willing to make the sacrifices required to help him. Go to Moscow and deal with the system, the infrastructure and the club.

When the fear factor is evident, one must have the heart of a lion.

I got a taxi out to the RZD Arena, which was the home stadium of Locomotiv Moscow, and when I got out of the car, there were two huge guys standing at the main door in suits and big coats.

Who the hell they were, I had no idea, but they stared at me like I was about to invade their territory.

Now was the time to be completely Albanian.

I stretched to my full height and stared back at them before seeking admittance to the stadium.

I was the representative of Garry O'Connor, and they were obliged to give me access to the directors of the club whether they liked it or not.

I was forceful without being threatening but they absolutely knew I meant every word that I said.

In that moment, we switched roles. They were used to being Russian and dominating western Europeans, but I flipped that over so that it was *they* who felt west European and I, Russian!

It was a battle of nerve, and I was determined that mine would hold.

I was admitted into the RZD and had my meeting.

However, even that narrative was changing as I was now being told that the original price of £3 million pounds had doubled.

This I needed in writing so that I could take it back to Steve Bruce and the chief executive at Birmingham City at that time, Karren Brady.

Birmingham had already had two bids of £1 million and £2 million rejected and I knew they would not treble that second bid.

It would all have to be negotiated.

And so I returned to the UK and went directly to see what could be done at Birmingham to get this deal done.

The club agreed to a final bid of £2.7 million and I transmitted that information to Lokomotiv.

That was when the interesting bit happened. I was sitting in the dining room of my hotel when someone arrived at my table.

He was French and came across as well-educated.

I had never met him before.

Anyway, I was just about to eat my dinner when this guy says to me, *Listen, Rudi. I have to be a part of this deal.*

I was amazed.

Where had he come from?

What was his angle?

Did he work for Birmingham City?

'But,' I countered; 'I have gone to Moscow on my own, faced down these people and I am close to making the deal for Garry and the club.'

He remained impassive and said, 'No. This is how it works. Without me there is no deal.'

I stared hard at him and spoke deliberately.

'Are you telling me that I have spent time preparing my dinner, sourcing the ingredients, working hard to cook it and now, when I am just about to eat it, you are taking it from me and eating it all to yourself?'

He shrugged his shoulders.

'That is how it works.'

I was extremely pissed off.

It was Rudi Vata who had gone off to Russia on his own.

Rudi Vata who had come out of the airport to be met by some scar-faced Chechens and their dubious taxi drivers.

Rudi Vata who had faced down 'security' at the RDZ Arena.

And Rudi Vata who had come away with the potential to make a deal to help Garry O'Connor out of a spot and help Birmingham City get the striker they craved.

And now, this Johnny-come-lately character was telling me that he had to be involved in a deal in which he had absolutely no active or practical participation.

I was now *more* than pissed off. I was extremely angry!

But, and this was critical – I could not lose my self-control.

I picked up my fork, pointed it at him and chose my words carefully.

'You know,' I said, 'you are a very lucky guy. You think that I am some ignorant Albanian and that you are well-educated. You are a very lucky guy.'

He stared back at me, but I could see he was trying to weigh me up.

'You are a lucky guy because I choose to tolerate you and it is you who are ignorant and I who am well-educated. The Rudi of 20 years ago? The Rudi who was not as well-educated as today? That Rudi would have taken this fork in my hand ...'

I held it up.

'... this fork ... and I would have used it to take your eyes out and put them on my plate because you have pissed me off.'

His mouth opened and I could see that I had struck a chord.

'You come in here after I have worked to prepare my meal – got together the ingredients, put the time in and am ready to enjoy it – and you insist that you are taking the plate from me.'

His mouth was still open, but he understood perfectly well.

*'Do not piss off an Albanian, my friend.'*

* * *

An arrangement was reached eventually with Karren Brady and Birmingham City, but not before I had phoned Garry to tell him that we should not be making this move happen.

Garry?

He begged me to do the deal so, in the end, I agreed to it.

This Johnny-come-lately would pick up his annual agency fee and I would have Garry's image rights which, in conclusion was, perhaps, a better deal, but it left a bitter taste in my mouth.

What did I say about football agency work?

The bigger the deal, the bigger the shark!

I started to think that I would pull back from this sort of life and do my A & B coaching badges but there was an epilogue to the story of Garry's transfer to Birmingham City.

A few weeks after the deal went through, I had one of those anonymous calls that one hears about from someone claiming to represent the *News of the World* newspaper.

The caller was quickly to the point.

Garry O'Connor and a team-mate had been caught on camera with some prostitutes in the Birmingham hotel where he was staying.

To avoid publication, this guy was looking for a fee of £20,000!

I thought he was bluffing but I phoned Garry right away.

He told me that it wasn't him who had invited these girls, it was his team-mate.

I raged at him.

*Garry – you begged me to get you away from Russia. You told me that you missed your family, your boy – and now you do this???*

I will say this. Garry was a cool one.

He refused to pay a penny and the *News of the World* ran with the story, but he didn't seem to care.

Me?

I was saddened.

CHAPTER 20

# FRIENDS AND ENEMIES

In order to get my coaching badges, I had to go back to Albania.

The football authorities in my country could authorise me to train and receive my A and B badges, which were the absolute minimum requirement if I ever wanted to coach in any country around the world.

I cannot say that I definitely wanted to go into management or, indeed, to become a coach but I did feel that the badges were a qualification I should have. You always have to be prepared for any eventuality in this life.

The way it worked was that the Albanian Football Federation had an arrangement with their counterparts in the Italian FA and so they would hire a couple of top technical directors to take us through the course.

Once completed, I would have a licence that was officially recognised by both FIFA and UEFA.

However, the chance at management came along quicker than I could ever have anticipated.

By the winter of 2011, my home team Vllaznia Shkoder were not in the best of places.

The club had not won the title in ten years and only had the Albanian Cup in 2008 as any form of silverware.

There was a smell of corruption around the place.

It all seemed to start going wrong when club president Myftar Cela was murdered in 2003 whilst in Montenegro. He took two shots in the head allegedly from a spurned business associate. His death was a stunning loss to the city and the club. Cela was much loved by the support because of his passion for the team and he was very generous to the club.

In 2006, an Albanian businessman by the name of Valter Fushaj took over as president. He did not seem to command the love of the supporters in the way Myftar Cela did and was caught up in a situation after a league game against Skenderbeu Korce in 2010.

Vllaznia won 3-2 but fielded an unlisted player, Ansi Nika and, as a consequence, the Albanian Football Federation declared the game a 2-0 win for Skenderbeu.

The fans erupted in fury, pointing a finger at Fushaj and others at the club, accusing them of bribery.

Incredibly, in that ten-year period, the club had gone through 20 managers in various forms.

Some were full-time – others were caretakers.

In that winter of 2011, I was out in Shkoder to see my parents.

The club had recently sacked their latest manager, Mirel Josa, after a poor run of form. Mirel was a distinguished former player who had spent the majority of his career with 17 Nentori and was also an Albanian international.

His assistant, Elvis Plori, a Shkoder native and former Vllaznia player, was in temporary charge and the club were looking for a new manager.

Valter Fushaj had moved on as well and the new president was also the mayor of the town, Lorenc Luka.

In a casual conversation, a local journalist named Gasper Marku, whom I knew well, had informed Luka that I was in town, and would he be interested in having a conversation with me about taking over as manager?

This was news to me, of course, but I must say, I was interested when I received the approach.

This was my hometown club, the place where it had all begun for me. I did, of course, have reservations.

The club were mid-table at that point and their recent history of managerial appointments made for a lengthy list.

However, the A and B badges had ignited something in me, and I now felt hungry enough to try my hand at coaching and so, after some lengthy and detailed discussions, I accepted the post.

I had told Luka that I would do an honest job and he took me at my word as well as promising to back me when it came to bringing new players into the club.

The facilities were not the best, but I knew what I could bring to the club – passion.

That was absolutely key to me. Not an uncontrolled passion but a structured one that had focus to it.

I wanted to develop the young players and provide a platform for them to advance their careers and bring success to the club.

Naturally, this would take time, but in my opinion, Vllaznia Shkoder should be a top-three team in Albania, competing in all domestic competitions and looking to get a foothold in the European game. Ambition. That was what was required.

The budget was tight, and we could not even afford to bring in an assistant for me.

There was an Italian guy who I had got to know really well. His name was Antonio, he had a good background in football and I felt he and I were on the same wavelength when we discussed the game and how it should be played.

He was good with the youths, had brought some young players through for Crystal Palace and I felt we were a natural fit together, but it was not to be.

That was a great shame as any manager, especially a new one, needs that one guy he can trust to go to when advice and counsel are required.

That second set of eyes and ears around the place, watching the players and, on occasion, intervening as a bridge between the dressing room and the manager.

In other words, someone who, in Glaswegian, '*has yer jaicket*'.

I was on my own.

Rudi against the system.

The hardest thing, of course, was having to leave Annfrances and my young boys back in Scotland, but I felt I needed to see how the job was going before I uprooted them and took them all to another country.

I studied my players.

Some of them were clearly honest battlers and I felt I could work with that.

I sat them down and told them how I operated.

I demanded hard work and endeavour as basic principles.

Just as in my own playing career, discipline would be paramount. Discipline of the mind and the body.

I promised to work on their fitness, which I did not think was optimum at that point, but we could get to that very quickly if they applied themselves.

And, of course, just like that first-team meeting with Tommy Burns when he took over at Celtic, I assured them that they would all get a fair chance to prove themselves to me and the support.

The training ground would be our sanctuary. That would be the place to do our best work and prepare for upcoming matches, but I warned them, do not bring any personal problems on to the training pitch.

As a group, we could not allow our focus to stray to matters of health, finance, wellbeing, the needs of our family et cetera when we were at our day job.

We started training at ten o'clock and I expected everyone to be there well before that as I had no time for latecomers.

I always felt a lack of care for the clock indicated a sloppiness about an individual and there was no room for that in my team.

We had to focus, work hard and, above all, give everything to the club and the support.

In other words, be serious about our jobs.

They all seemed to agree with me, and I felt good once I had outlined my plans to them. Naturally, there could be the odd rotten apple or two, but I would just have to work that out for myself.

Of course, there were no new players as promised by Lorenc Luka.

I suppose that should not have been a surprise. After all, he was, first and foremost, a politician and that is generally a species I do not have a great deal of time for with their casual use of power to get what they want.

I would just have to work with the squad that I had at my disposal. We started well. In the first two games we beat Apolonia, who had just been promoted the season before, 4-1 and followed that up with a 3-3 draw against Bylis.

Seven goals scored and four out of a possible seven points gained.

I was quite pleased with the way the players were initially responding to my methods and then, I encountered a problem.

Our next fixture was a home game against Skenderbeu and, at the time, they were probably the best team in the country who would, in fact, go on to lift the title.

It was as tough a match as we could get and a real test of the side.

We booked into a hotel two days prior to the match and set up our camp right there.

By now, the players had a very clear picture of what I was about. I was a leader. I lead, they follow.

On the day of the match, I had made preparations down to the last detail. The pre-match team talk would be about three and a half hours before kick-off.

This was a critical time. I had set up a tactics board and would be outlining my plans for the game.

The boys all arrived and filed into the meeting, but before anything, before team talks and tactics, I needed to look at every one of them individually, right into their eyes.

I needed to see that energy.

Who would be standing up for me, for the support, for Vllaznia Shkoder? When you look into a player's eyes in those moments, you are looking for fire, not fear.

Are you ready?

Do you have what it takes?

How much do you want this?

And I could see it as I moved along the line of each of my players – and then I got to Xhevahir Sukaj, who was a striker.

I liked him.

The boy had potential and I had gone so far as to suggest to the Albanian Football Federation that they should look at him again as he had only made one appearance for his country up until that point.

Xhevahir had just turned 24 and was a young man from Shkoder who had come through the academy system to play for the first team.

For one so young he had, astonishingly, played for six clubs as well as this, his third spell at Vllaznia. There had been a couple of outright transfers and a few loan spells, but six clubs were a lot in such a short period of time.

It suggested to me that there was, perhaps, a fragility about the boy although I could confidently say that he was one of my best players.

Set pieces, free kicks, corners, Xhevahir would be involved in them all and he could score goals as well.

He would be one of the guys I would be counting on to test the Skenderbeu back line but now, as I stepped up to him, he turned his eyes away from me!

I confronted him – forced him to look me in the face.

*Xhevahir – are you ready to play?*

I needed him to say 'yes'.

He stared blankly at me and then said, *No.*

I could not believe what I was hearing but I needed an explanation.

He told me that the club owed him money.

A signing-on fee of some $10,000.

They had promised it to him on the day he had signed, and they had not given him it. I thought back, of course, to the promises of player recruitment from the club president that had not materialised either.

Apparently, the latest news was that he was to receive the money on the previous Monday, and this was now the day of the match and he had still not been paid.

I had no time for this.

I had told the players that they never bring this sort of shit to the team or the training ground and now, here it was, spilling over into a matchday and only three and a half hours before kick-off.

In all my time in the game, I had never experienced this before – a player saying that he was not ready for the game.

'Listen,' I said. 'You have two minutes to tell me that you are ready.'

And I timed it as he sat in silence.

All the while I thought, *Please God, make him realise that he cannot do this to us at this time.*

It was a matter for the financial administrators at the club, or the president. It was certainly not a matter for the manager who was only focused on one thing – putting a team out on the park ready to go into battle with a top side.

I counted down the last 30 seconds on my watch and asked him again.

'Xhevahir – are you ready to play?'

There was a brief moment of silence before he answered.

*I will let you know when we get to the stadium.*

Here now was a moment.

A test.

What kind of a leader was I in front of my troops?

If I was prepared to back down on this and re-draft my plans at the stadium to perhaps accommodate a rankled and unsettled player, then where would that leave me? Where would that leave my credibility with my squad?

It was very simple – there was only one response.

I stood my ground.

'No' I said. 'Stand up and get out of this room.'

Xhevahir looked a bit shocked but did as I told him and now, I had to re-plan my thinking on the match.

What was I to do?

I could not stand there and have a player relate to me his terms for his co-operation with me and his team-mates.

I knew in that instant that I had made the right choice – the only choice.

The choice that managers like Tommy Burns, Eduard Geyer and Pierre Littbarski would have made.

Not only had I made that choice – I also suspended the player.

We played well that day but lost 2-0.

There are always so many ifs and buts in a football match, but it's certainly an argument that a player with the qualities of Xhevahir Sukaj could have made a material difference out on the pitch.

Then again, with his mental approach, who can say?

I took a risk.

In my opinion, a *necessary* risk and, furthermore, he never played for me again.

I had to set an example to my players.

No matter what is going on in your private life, no one person is bigger than the club.

There followed a two-week pattern when I was pressurised by certain people at the club, directors, administrators to welcome Xhevahir back into the fold.

'You must forgive him,' they said. 'He is one of our best players.'

'I have forgiven him,' I would answer. 'But *football* has not forgiven him.'

They didn't like that, of course.

Only my third game in and I was leaving out a star player on a point of principle.

As directors, I felt they had not been used to that kind of discipline around the club. I could relate, in part, to what this young man was going through. I had been there at that period when I had come back to Albania and SK Tirana.

Metwally El Sayed had promised me a signing-on fee and had reneged on that promise, but I had not let it affect my game.

I would not allow it to create an avenue where I would short-change my team-mates or supporters of the club.

It had to be put to one side and negotiated away from a matchday.

Yes, it soured my relationship with the Egyptian and I had moved on, but I could put it out of my mind on those days when I had to focus on the game.

The decision I had made on Xhevahir had been a necessary one and I had made it to be real. To be different.

To survive.

Now the players had seen my example and that I wasn't just all about words. I took decisive action because that's what a leader does, and I was glad that they had seen me do so.

However, undoubtedly now there would be people behind the scenes at the club who would have it in for me.

There were friends – but there were also enemies.

* * *

I sold Xhevahir Sukaj in the January of 2012.

He moved to Iran and a top tier club, Sepahan SC, who would go to win the title that season. It was a good move for Sukaj – a good move for Sepahan – and I know that Vllaznia Shkoder did well financially from the deal.

In addition, the club had sold another of my players, attacking midfielder Armando Vajushi, to Bulgarian champions Litex Lovech whilst I was back in Scotland seeing my family. This was not a deal I had approved. The boy was only 20 years of age, and I viewed him as a prospect.

The money was good for both players, but I needed the funds to replace both of them and the transfer window was closing at the end of the month.

I had submitted the names of some players whom I thought would make a difference to our team, but they were never acted upon.

We were still a team in transition and the lack of new players and, indeed, the input of some of the older players, whom I felt were not contributing, meant that I was having to play young boys in midfield. It takes time to build a team, to develop characters and personalities and although I felt I was making the right choices, I was not stupid.

I could tell that the ground was moving underneath me.

We got through to April and had a big match coming up away to Pogradeci which entailed a bit of a journey.

I had been hearing rumours about match fixing, even from within our own ranks. I had no proof, never had the facts, but those rumours were as thick as smoke and not easy to dispel.

Pogradeci were not having a good season and were struggling against relegation.

Despite our ongoing problems with squad unrest and having to blood youngsters, we had remained consistent and at that stage were looking up at potential European competition qualification as opposed to down and the relegation play-offs.

When I had first arrived at the club and discussed budget, I was told, as I recall, that a certain portion of that budget had to be set aside for referees.

A required fund to influence decisions and matches.

This meeting, to the best of my recollection, had taken place in the presence of two club directors, although I cannot recall who had suggested this 'black fund' for referees.

This shocked me.

Again, I had heard rumours but to have it spelt out to me was staggering.

'If you can buy matches, then you do not need a manager,' I said.

'Everybody does it,' I was told.

'We do not deal with the referees, and we do not *have* to deal with the referees,' I retorted.

By that April, I knew that my contract was not being renewed.

I still retained the support of the honest supporters who could see the job that I was trying to do but I had railed against the system and now the system wanted its revenge upon me.

The match against Pogradeci drew a line in the sand for me.

We had goals that we considered to be legitimate being chalked off for 'offside' by the referee and, if that was not enough, one of my players scored an own goal.

We lost 2-1 and the fact that Pogradeci still got relegated at the end of the season was of little consequence to me.

There seemed no point in arguing that the referee had been 'bought', as was so eloquently pointed out to me by those directors way back in that first meeting that I had with them when I took the manager's job on in November.

The day after the defeat by Pogradeci, I called a press conference to which written and visual media were invited.

It was time to expose the corruption at the heart of our game in Albania and, indeed, those at Vllaznia Shkoder.

I had prepared 19 points where I thought Vllaznia Shkoder was being run to the financial and sporting detriment of the club and, equally, I expressed the belief that the Albanian Football Federation were complicit in the level of corruption that was going on in the game and were not prepared to do anything about it.

The effect of all this was seismic to the press, both sporting and political, in the country.

No one had ever come out and questioned the integrity of the Albanian Football Federation, but this was how it was, in my opinion. Football and politics were no different.

They were dependent on each other and, in my view, politicians such as Lorenc Luka were only using Vllaznia Shkoder to further their political ambitions and garner votes for themselves.

Luka himself wanted me to retract a statement I had made regarding the 'black fund' but I would not do so.

After an emergency meeting held by the club supervisory board on the following day, I was dismissed from my position as club coach – which came as no surprise to me.

That was when all hell broke loose, and the media were caught up in the story.

The club issued a statement.

To summarise, they stated that I had prepared my briefing in a 'non-professional and unethical manner, loaded with low defamation, anger and malice towards Vllaznia Shkoder, in order to damage the image of the club.'

Furthermore, they demanded an apology from me.

I refused and when they threatened legal action, I reiterated to them that I was willing to go to court, repeat my comments and defend both my words and my reputation.

In response to their threats, I issued my own statement which was reported in the media as follows:

> I can say I haven't made any accusations. I only told the facts. I am one of those people who tells the truth. I hope justice is introduced as soon as possible and investigates everything that happens in Albania and in Albanian football. I wish and want to address the justice of Vllaznia as soon as possible and Rudi Vata as a just person, as a citizen of Albania, is ready to face all those people who are deified and are familiar with their image that they have built.

I knew I was a threat.

A threat to the corrupt politicians and their politics that had no time for the people but was interested only in their own self-value.

I also had to state a case for football. Nobody had the right to take this beautiful game of ours and cheat it out of existence.

I have already stated that I would have died for the game, and I knew that I was at risk of being shot, but once again, I had to stand my ground.

The Albanian Football Federation got involved as well. They could hardly fail to do so and were more animated about my views on the bribery of match officials which I felt was common practice throughout the country.

They too issued a statement. The allegations would be forwarded to the legal committees in the federation for consideration where it most likely become a disciplinary investigation.

I thought that was one of those classic authoritarian statements that was kicking a can further down the road with absolutely no intention of any action that would expose what was actually going on in the game.

There would be political stalemate on all of this and Vllaznia never followed up on their threats to take me to court.

Me? I was proud. I had done my duty – my duty to the game.

It saddened me that there would be no change, but that was political life in Albania.

I wanted my country to really enter the European stage both political and sporting, but I guess small-minded, short-term corruption would always be in the forefront to prevent that happening for my people.

We had come a long way, but we had a longer road to travel.

* * *

For most of the next few years, I continued to work in the football agency field and then an opportunity arose at the latter stages of 2019.

Bernd Hollerbach was a German full-back with Hamburg SV whom I got to know well from my time playing with Energie Cottbus.

We were roughly the same age, got on well and had a mutual respect for each other.

When we talked about football, I felt we were on the same lines. He retired from the playing side around the same time I did and almost immediately went into coaching.

He started off at SV Hamburg and over the next decade or so, he worked at various clubs, mostly in Germany, in roles as assistant coach and head coach, for example with his hometown team, Wurzburger Kickers.

In the summer of 2019, he was invited to take over as manager at Belgian club Royal Excel Mouscron.

Coincidentally, I had played against Mouscron when I was in Cyprus with Apollon Limassol when we lost out on aggregate over two legs in that season's UEFA Cup competition.

I received a call one day from Bernd asking if I would fancy the role of sporting director at the club and it piqued my interest so I headed over to Belgium.

When I had played against them, back in 1997, they were officially known as Royal *Excelsior* Mouscron, but having gone bankrupt in 2009, they merged with RRC Peruwelz before renaming themselves Royal Excel Mouscron.

There was a turbulent period with various owners but when I took up the position, they were still operating in the top tier of the Belgian league.

At a meeting with the club, I outlined what I could do within their remit, which was to source new talent, new projects and bring them to the club for development.

At one point, they had a tie-in with French Ligue 1 club, Lille OSC, which was just about half an hour away across the border, but that had come to an end in 2015.

However, the suburbs of Lille and Paris would be where I would start to look for talent.

I produced a plan for the club, and it was very much a 'hands-on' project with me travelling extensively between Belgium and France.

To me, the rough diamonds were to be found in these tough suburbs of the cities.

Here now is where one would find young players who were not only looking to have a career in the game, but equally, have that hunger and desire to come out of these neighbourhoods.

I really enjoyed the job.

Development was always my thing, and I was able to bring some new, young talent into the club in a short period of time.

I thought back to all I had learned from my earliest days at Loro Borici school in Tirana when the influence of people such as coach Aurel Verria could shape the future path for a young player. I was not just looking for players who had skill on the ball and could read the game. As ever, I was looking for mentality, character, personality.

You could find that if you looked hard enough.

What was imperative for me, though, was to make sure any boy coming into the club would be well looked-after.

When you came into my office at Mouscron you would see my desk and, behind that, on the wall, were two pictures of Ruan and Rocco.

When people found out who were in the pictures, they often assumed I had them up on the wall as a reminder of my sons and my love for them both, but there was more to it than that.

When asked about it, I would reply: 'The pictures are there to remind me of the job I have to do, and a fundamental of that job is to look after every boy who comes into the club as well as I would look after my sons if they were here.'

That is what I would require of a sporting director, manager, coach, whoever. They need to look after the boys like they were their own.

Agents, naturally, would call me to say they had players to bring to the club but that was not always the way that it worked.

Some agents are not prepared to go into the tough suburbs to hew out talent, so I was more reliant on those scouts who were willing do so and followed my nose on that point.

Bernd and I worked well together, and I had genuine hopes for the partnership. He had a short illness around the January of 2020 and was absent for about a month. I helped out his academy director, Philippe Saint-Jean, with the players and I enjoyed that very much. I felt they were responding to us.

Bernd returned to active duty by the end of February. However, there was something in the air – Covid.

What can one say about the global pandemic?

I suppose, as with the majority of people around the world, it was impossible to comprehend what was going on.

There were words being bandied about a lot, like lockdown, shutdown and herd immunity.

It was a situation beyond our control and there was, potentially, a situation wherein I could be trapped in Belgium with no route to getting back to Annfrances and my boys in Scotland.

I had to get back.

Ultimately, in 2022, Royal Excel Mouscron were declared bankrupt, and the club ceased to exist, which was very sad for everybody involved.

There may have been financial irregularities or perhaps the lockdown had a terminal effect on the club's reserves as it did with a lot of businesses, but who can say for sure?

* * *

It seemed that my past life with Celtic was not quite past when I was approached after the lockdown period by a guy called Nick Hammond who, at the time, was overseeing the scouting role at the club.

He called me, at the behest, I believe, of Peter Lawwell, who was about to retire from his role as chief executive officer at Celtic. Peter and I knew each other from the times when I had come over to Celtic and, of course, my son Rocco had signed for the club, which I will capture in the next chapter.

To my understanding, Peter had urged Nick to get in touch with me.

When I had retired in 2004, I used to go to watch Celtic and Tommy Burns would get me tickets for the matches.

Through Tommy, I was introduced to Peter, and we had a mutual respect, I feel, for each other.

That, perhaps, is why he said to Nick to reach out to me.

The approach was made and, for about eight months, I did some work for the club in a scouting capacity.

There is an online system called *Wyscout* which contains many videos of players and Celtic would send me about five or six players a week to assess.

I enjoyed the work. I would sit down with my laptop and watch the players going about their business.

One day, they sent me a video of a Tottenham Hotspur player who was out on loan at Bournemouth.

The boy had come through the Tottenham academy but had never played a first-team game for the club.

In fact, over a four-year period, he had been bounced about many clubs with various loan deals.

I knew how difficult it could be at a top English club.

Teams like Tottenham, Arsenal, Chelsea et cetera had many players on their books from academy right through to main squad and it was difficult to get a place in the first team.

I watched videos of this guy and liked what I saw.

He appeared to be solid, reliable and, although a centre-back, had an ability to play out through midfield and take the ball forward.

I recommended that Celtic bring the boy in, even if it was just a loan deal initially.

His name was Cameron Carter-Vickers and, as I write this book, he has become a mainstay at Celtic Football Club.

With his help, and under two managers, Ange Postecoglou and Brendan Rodgers, he has won the Scottish Premiership three times, picked up two Scottish Cups and two Scottish League Cups in three years as well as playing in the World Cup for his country, the United States of America.

That's not a bad return on the investment, is it?

## CHAPTER 21

# MY BOYS

When I retired from playing in 2004, I found time to do something that I had wanted to do for quite a while.

As you may recall, my maternal grandmother, Jelena, originally came from Montenegro and had to make that heart-breaking decision in 1946 to abandon the country of her birth and raise her children in Albania.

I decided I wanted to connect with Montenegro as my roots were there as well as in the country of my birth.

We still had family cousins in the country.

I asked a friend of mine if he could look out for a house for me.

There were certain criteria attached to this request, which included a view of the sea and plenty of space around us.

This wasn't just for me and Annfrances, of course. With Rocco on the way, I wanted to have a place where I could take my boys in the summer.

Somewhere that we could spend a few months away from Scotland in the sunshine.

Just like the upbringings that Aleks and I had, I wanted the boys surrounded by the beauties of nature in all its brilliance and that included fruits, figs and berries.

It took a while, but after viewing close to 30 properties, we eventually decided on one that had everything we wanted and so I made the purchase.

I have never regretted that decision.

The villa was on a hilltop just outside of the beautiful coastal town of Ulcinj which has been described as a 'gem on the Adriatic coast' – and it really is.

We had a magnificent view right across the bay and out into the sea; no neighbours, so plenty of privacy; and were situated just 40 kilometres from my parents across the border in Shkoder.

We had it all.

Sea. Peace of mind. Security.

The boys would wander around in their bare feet, clad only in t-shirts and shorts for the whole summer.

At time of writing, my boys are now 22 and 19, and they have both spent so much time in Montenegro with, hopefully, more to come.

It has been the ideal place for us to base ourselves over the holiday periods and we have even managed to have the odd winter break there as well.

Here, also, was a place where the boys could meet lots of other kids of their age but from different countries, different cultures.

They have made friends with boys and girls from Serbia, Russia, Ukraine and more.

It seemed that every time I looked out of the window, there were kids milling around the pool area.

It is a big part of their education, in my opinion.

Interacting with others is always a way to better understand the world and the people in it.

Parenthood has been the biggest responsibility of my life.

I really believe that.

My own parents provided both me and Aleks with more than just a roof above our heads. They also gave us the bricks and mortar to build our own lives.

That was what I wanted for my boys.

It was important for both Annfrances and myself that they understood their heritage and the roots they both have and not just in Albania.

Annfrances has *her* roots in Ireland as well as Scotland.

Her mother, Ann Brown, was born in the peninsular coastal village of Howth in the county of Dublin.

I think that is such a rich vein in the DNA of my boys – a mix of the Balkans and the Celtic nations!

It has also allowed my younger son to represent the Republic of Ireland at a junior level, but a bit more on that later.

The boys have always been close, and I fervently hope that will always be the case. We have specifically raised them that way.

Of course, they are different people.

Ruan is more of a thinker and has a keen brain for finance and figures. You could see that in him from an early age.

He likes his sport, played football, swims brilliantly and also boxes.

Rocco was always addicted to his football and, as a child, seemed to permanently have a ball at his feet.

From young, you could see that he had an unbelievable balance about him, and I have videos taken in lockdown where he is standing on a football in his bare feet without falling off.

Balance, to me, is absolutely critical when it comes to playing football.

I seem to recall hearing a theory that suggested the reason why Brazilian players had such gifted balance was their mothers would dance the samba whilst carrying them in the womb!

It does seem a bit far-fetched, but one never knows!

Rocco's route into football started when he was six at a club called Mill United who are based in Hamilton.

The club prides itself on promoting the game at grassroots level although, as I recall, they were not keen to give Rocco a trial at first.

They said they had no space for him.

It took the intervention of one of the mothers of another young boy at the club who badgered a coach to look at him.

Five minutes into his trial, the coach wanted him at the club.

It was obvious that he had talent, but he also had that other vital ingredient – work rate.

Throughout this book, I have always stressed the need to work – to express yourself.

Nothing ever came easy to Rudi Vata, and I had to work for everything that I desired in life.

It's also important to be yourself.

Be comfortable in your own skin and be the best version of you that you can be.

Like many boys of his age, Rocco's biggest hero out on the pitch when he was growing up was the Argentinian, Lionel Messi.

And no wonder!

Gifted, mercurial and, above all, balanced, the diminutive South American can do it all and has won everything the game has to offer. Eight times the FIFA Ballon d'Or winner, four UEFA Champions League titles and, of course, the biggest of the lot, the World Cup.

As a player, you could have no better idol.

One day, when he was ten, Rocco said to me, 'Dad, I want to change my name to Rocco Messi.'

What could a father say?

It reminded me of the 1974 World Cup all over again and that brilliant Dutch side with Johan Cruyff, Johan Neeskens, Johnny Rep and, of course, my *own* hero, Ruud Krol.

I thought back to when I wrote his name inside my state-provided school bag, risking the wrath of my father and his rational fear that I could get into serious trouble with the authorities for wanting to emulate Ruud Krol.

I just had to settle for the fact that we both shared a common first name. He was Ruud and I was Rudi – that was enough for me.

I said to Rocco, 'When Lionel Messi was your age, he would be just like you. Loving his football. Dreaming and planning for a career in the game. Playing for a top club, representing his country and all of that based on being the best version of Lionel Messi that he could be – that is all you can do, son.'

He looked at me and we left it at that for the time being but the very next day he came back to me and said, 'Dad – I have changed my mind. I want to become Rocco VATA.'

Be the best version of you that you can be.

I felt it was important not to spoil my boys.

That could be difficult with Ruan as the first born.

It can be very easy to overdo it with your first child and not just yourself but others in the family as well.

When we came home from Japan at Christmas 2003, Annfrances and I decided not to be overly lavish with toys and presents for Ruan and urged that of the family as well.

Start as you mean to go on.

It's not about being miserable. It's about reining it in when things can get out of hand, and you must have some discipline.

Consequently, I believe Ruan has grown up with a balanced view of life.

As I said, he is more of a thinker.

He had talent as a footballer as well but just not that little bit extra that perhaps would have propelled him into the game as a career.

He has an astute brain and is very interested in financial affairs. He takes *his* risks in the stock market and formulates his plans based on the information that he gleans from his computer.

Rocco is more of a risk-taker in sport and can be fearless.

We have a swimming pool out in Montenegro, and it is deep enough for one to dive in from the side of the pool.

But Rocco discovered the high wall that is situated a few feet away from the pool and he would climb up it and then launch himself beyond the side of the pool and into the water.

Equally, like Ruan, his brain worked in a certain way.

I remember one time when my father was visiting us, and he was sitting with a sheet of paper and a pencil.

My father had enjoyed a bit of a career in house building as well as his other accomplishments and this day, he was using his architect's mind to sketch out some lines.

He was astonished when Rocco, who was just a wee boy at the time, barely in school, picked up another pencil and copied my dad, line for line, in perfect harmony!

'What is this?' he would say to me, and I would just smile and shrug my shoulders.

Both boys are very fit, as you would expect.

Ruan is very big on nutrition.

He has always looked at what he is eating, and he trains like a boxer so therefore, he *eats* like a boxer.

Ruan shares this knowledge with his brother and helps him to prepare for his football.

It was obvious, as I say, that Rocco had talent and, given my connections in the world of football and, naturally enough, with Celtic, people often encouraged me to contact the club's academy and urge them to look at Rocco.

This I would not do.

I always felt that if he had that much talent then a club would discover him, naturally.

I do know that the father of my great friend, Paul McStay, who scouted for Celtic, to watch Rocco play and this maybe is how he ended up at the Celtic academy.

He pretty much went there straight from Mill United at seven years of age.

The club have looked after him, nurtured him and he rewarded them with his development through the ranks up until the age of 16 when he signed a pre-contract agreement with Celtic.

Here now was a new chapter in his football life and, naturally, a very proud day for me, Annfrances and Ruan.

His development was such that the club contacted us one day, when he was around 14 years of age, to say that there had been an enquiry from the Football Association of Ireland to see if he would be interested in joining up with them.

Rocco, of course, qualifies to play for the Republic of Ireland as well as Scotland and Albania. That rich mix of the Balkans and the Celts, again.

There may even be a case for including Montenegro in that mix given my own heritage through my grandmother, but Ireland were the first to express their interest.

He asked me what I thought, and I told him to go and enjoy these new experiences.

Work with new people and get stronger.

The FAI had done their homework on Rocco and were delighted when he agreed to go with them.

On a personal note, Annfrances and I liked it as well.

She, obviously, has that deep-rooted Irish connection, but I also liked the fact that Celtic were founded by an Irishman – Brother Walfrid, a Marist Brother from Ballymote, Sligo.

Any visitor to Celtic Park is greeted by a statue of the man outside the ground, so that little piece of Ireland will always be in the club's DNA.

For Rocco Vata of Celtic to become Rocco Vata of the Republic of Ireland seemed like a natural fit.

The Irish set-up has been very good for him and a definite plus in his development. It's funny, in a way, that the FAI knocked on our door when he was 14.

It reminded me of Rudi Vata at 14 and that journey to Tirana – to the place where I was almost to become like an orphan.

Cut off from my family and on my own.

I had to grow, learn, and mature in a difficult environment but that was when my development started.

The Rudi who went on to play at an elite level for his country had his start in Tirana.

It's not an exact parallel with my son but there are similarities.

He had to adapt very quickly to a different environment and interact with others in their development as well as his own.

The grounding would be there and now he would have to have those three qualities that I always looked for in other players, other managers.

Mentality.

Character.

Personality.

Both my boys have those qualities and Annfrances and I have always tried to instil that in them.

Do not be afraid to face any challenge.

You are building a house and start with the foundations.

Once they are in place, you can move on to develop and shape the frame of your house.

Get that done and you can put a roof on that house before kitting out the various rooms of your life.

Do not make excuses.

Do not complain.

Just get on with it.

Excuses can weaken you. They can soften you up when the reality is that you have to face your fears and overcome them.

During the pandemic, Rocco arrived with an apparatus that I was to build up for him.

It was basically a machine to allow him to do dips and pull-ups and was simple to construct.

Before heading off to training at Lennoxtown, after the relaxation of lockdown restrictions, he would do 25 dips and 25 pull-ups.

He told me that if he could do these exercises over 200 days then that would amount to 5,000 dips and 5,000 pull-ups a year.

That is the kind of thinking you have to have if you want to be an elite athlete.

Both he and Ruan train like boxers and it's very rewarding for us to see them together, helping each other out.

As I said before, parenthood has been one of the biggest responsibilities in my life and I like to think that between us, Annfrances and I have given both Ruan and Rocco the bricks and mortar to start building their *own* respective houses.

Only time and the fates will tell, of course, but we have done as much as we can, and God has allowed us to do much for our boys.

And, of course, in God we trust.

CHAPTER 22

# TWO LIVES

*'In a sense, when I look at my life, I sometimes feel as if I have lived* ***two*** *lives in one existence.'*

On occasion, when I have been speaking to various people over the years recalling the story of my life, they have remarked that I should get all this down on paper and that is perhaps the reason I have undertaken to do that now.

The expression that I set out prior to the prologue and that starts this final chapter has been a cornerstone of my life.

I *do* feel that I have lived two lives in one existence and the Rudi Vata of today is not the Rudi Vata of, say, 35 years ago.

I suppose that may be true of most of us.

The great span of my life has taken me through austerity, communism, state-controlled bureaucracy, and a powerful quest for freedom in the first part of my story. As you have read over those early chapters, to even *dream* of freedom would have been deemed a crime in that 45-year period of 1946–91 in Albania.

I felt I was like most young people of the day – carefree, happy, desirous of what the future could bring, but in my case, wary of the various traps that I could perhaps land in were I not careful in how I conducted myself in public.

That incident from 1987 when, I felt, me and my family came perilously close to banishment still sends a chill through me.

That was the way of totalitarianism. No recourse. No opportunity to refute charges pointed at you from anonymous sources.

One lived with the capriciousness of a state official, in my case, the Minister of the Interior, Hekuran Isai.

I have always believed that the next part of my life started with his signature on a document that I was never to see. But I understood, very clearly, that it existed.

From then on, I dedicated myself to my craft, my sport: in a sense, my deliverance.

Football has been the constant in my life from the barefoot soil days of my childhood right through to the end of my playing career in 2004.

I would have died for the game.

Dinamo Tirana were the team that 'blooded' me. The team that allowed me to believe that I could have a career in the game, albeit given the mediocrity of the wage structure, one that would require a parallel career which, at the time, I thought would be as a physical education teacher then, at a later point, coaching.

At that stage of my life, I could not have conceived of playing my domestic football outside of Albania.

Yes, there was the potential for European competition, the Balkan Cup, and international football that could take you overseas, but the day-to-day routine was as set in stone as it could be, and I understood that concept.

As young Albanians, we would never be allowed out of the country unless accompanied by *'state officials'*, the dreaded *Sigurimi*.

The sniff of freedom that playing for one's country could offer would remain just that, unless one was willing to risk everything, including retribution against those left behind.

Which brings me to a part of my profession that I have not addressed in any great detail throughout this book and that was my international career.

Growing up in Albania with football as my calling, the goal would always have been to represent my country and I was proud to do so for the very first time on 30 May 1990 in a friendly in Reykjavik against Iceland.

We lost 2-0 but the sensation of pulling that red jersey over my head felt like a pivotal moment and yet, I did realise after my second match, the famous one out in Paris on the night that I sought political asylum, that I would, in all likelihood, never play for my country again.

That decision had to be taken in context. I was choosing freedom – a completely new way of life – and so, I had to wrestle with my conscience about the choices I was making.

It was a guarantee that I would not be selected by the old regime, having chosen to defect to another country.

Suffice to say, I was more than happy when Bejkush Birce called me back into his squad for the World Cup qualifying match against Spain in April 1992.

I returned to that squad a different man, an independent man and was willing to share my new experiences with my team-mates. Even I, though, could not have foreseen the new experiences that were waiting for *me* after the next game for my country, in Dublin against the Republic of Ireland.

Not for the first time, I would discover how one's life can change rapidly with those little margins.

The fact that Liam Brady was in the stadium that day.

The fact that, as the manager of Celtic, he would not just have been there as an interested spectator, but as someone who would be taking in every game he could, looking for talent.

Let's not forget that other margin when the Albanian national physiotherapist asked me casually sometime later, when he was working on my body, about what had happened to the interest that Scottish club Celtic had shown in me.

It is a racing certainty that I would never have headed to Glasgow had I not forced the issue on the back of this information.

Old habits may age, but they never changed with the Albanian Football Federation.

Incidentally, the background to that match in Dublin provided an interesting, and yet typical of its time, prelude to the fixture that I think was widely reported in the press.

Albanian football was struggling to keep up with costs in a country where the standard of living, economy and wages were dropping as in that period of transition. There was little enough to go around and, when we arrived in Ireland after two stops and a 15-hour journey, we were already a depleted squad and had no balls, training or medical equipment – or strips.

We would be forced to play some under-21s again in the first team but the whole issue of whether the game could take place hung in the air.

A loan from the Olympic Council and a very welcome donation, for some unexplained reason, from the Spanish Football Association would cover our costs, but not having proper kit could be a determinant in the game being called off and the Republic of Ireland being given a forfeit.

I believe there was last-minute help from a branch of giant sportswear manufacturers adidas and an Irish local newspaper, which would allow for preparation of a kit.

The Football Association of Ireland also agreed to offset some of our costs.

So, all seemed well and good and then the old school politics kicked in.

The badge on our jerseys, denoting our country, had always been the same – a two-headed eagle resting on a red star to denote communism.

That red star had only just been removed at the behest of the Albanian Football Federation, so they made it clear; any kit going forward had to sport the new badge.

I can only imagine the headaches involved in trying to produce all this in such a short space of time and, in truth, it was clear that we would need to have similar help throughout the course of our campaign.

Under the circumstances– lack of resources, a first-team kit that did not arrive at the stadium until a couple of hours before kick-off, and having to introduce three under-21s into our starting 11 – it was somewhat of a miracle that we played so well to be in the game until the latter stages.

Or was it?

Perhaps all of those setbacks that I have just listed contributed to our resolution to play for our pride – and that is a primary motivating factor in life as well as in sport.

Perhaps, in my own case, it was this sense of pride that pushed me to play as well as I did *and* catch the attention of Liam Brady.

Who can honestly say?

I fulfilled a variety of roles for my country under five different managers. Generally, I was at centre-back, but I also operated on both sides of the defence, occasionally as sweeper and even patrolling the midfield when required.

From those positions, goals were never going to be abundant, but apart from, famously, that equaliser out in Hannover in 1997, I had scored the winner in a 3-2 Euros qualifier victory out in Moldova two years previously and also bagged the last three of my five international goals in friendlies against Macedonia, Andorra and Malta.

Albania were never going to be serious contenders, in those days, to advance to international tournaments such as the World Cup or the Euros, but given our depleted resources, we worked hard for our country.

The occasional triumph such as that night in 1993 when we beat Northern Ireland in Switzerland were good for raising morale as well as the reputation of our nation.

We were determined that the new Albania, the one struggling to gain some kind of democracy, such as it was, would not pay mere lip service to the international scene and none of us ever walked out on to a pitch with our heads low.

From the target of playing for my country, there was also the dream of *captaining* my country, which I had done at under-21 level before stepping up to the senior role between 1997-99.

To be shaking hands at the halfway line with my international counterparts was a great experience. Real leaders of men like Germany's Oliver Bierhoff, Jurgen Klinsmann, Oliver Kahn and Jurgen Kohler. From Portugal, the magnificent Luis Figo and the charismatic and talented Hristo Stoichkov of Bulgaria. You had to earn the respect of these guys.

I always felt the job of captain was not just about the 90 minutes out on the turf.

You were a role model, a catalyst, a leader for your teammates and the bridge between the manager and his squad.

The national team manager when I was his captain was Astrit Hafizi and his name has popped up a few times in my journey.

He was my first manager when I was a young man at Vllaznia Shkoder and, as I mentioned, when I was captain of Albania. In fact, it was he who asked me to assume the captaincy of my country in the first place.

Crucially, though, he was there for my father that day of the protests in Shkoder in 1991, just after I had defected to France and he it was who offered a shoulder to him when he was quietly sobbing about his boys leaving Albania.

That is the kind of man to take responsibility for an international football squad.

Playing for my country took me all over Europe, let me absorb different cultures and customs as well as seeing those parts of the world that a lot of my people would not have had access to or, sadly, could not afford.

I played my final international match on 1 September 2001, coming off the bench as a substitute in a 2-0 defeat at home to Finland in a World Cup qualifier.

The game took place in the old Qemal Stafa stadium in Tirana and so, once again, I had returned to the capital where my professional career got started.

Interestingly, a few years ago, the stadium was demolished and rebuilt so as to provide an arena that was standard to UEFA requirements for European competition.

In November 2019, the stadium re-opened and had a new name – the Arena Kombetare.

The name *Qemal Stafa* was thus erased from the sporting life of Albania and the wartime link to the fallen Partisan hero whose name had been honoured by the communists was gone.

To me, it was another sign of the changes in the new, modern Albania.

I played 58 times for my country over an 11-year period, and I believe I always gave good service to the badge and the people.

When I go back to Shkoder or visit Tirana, those people remember me as the captain of their country's team which, given that I spent the vast majority of my club career outside of Albania, is not a bad way to be remembered.

* * *

In saying that, a lot of the Albanian public may also recall that I played for Celtic in Glasgow as my move to Scotland from France was quite a story in the sporting press at the time.

Unquestionably, given their success and continental pedigree as European Cup winners in 1967, the club's name was well known even in the communist outposts of Albania, and their visit to play Partizani Tirana in 1979 was, as I said, a big event.

Several thousand actually turned out to watch the Celtic squad train on the day before the game.

It was the Irishman Liam Brady who gave me my opportunity in the West, and I will forever be grateful to him for that chance.

In Lou Macari, I felt, after an initially poor start between us, that I could work with him, but the reality was that he was not around long enough at Celtic Park for us to build an enduring working relationship.

Tommy Burns could be somewhat of an enigma to me at times.

I have already outlined my disappointing start to his tenure in charge, but I did come to love him. I arrived at the conclusion that he was an honest man who, without any question, was dedicated not just to the team and the football, but the club itself.

We shared the joy of a Scottish Cup win that was big for Rudi Vata as the first Albanian player to pick up a major domestic honour in Europe, but more importantly, was huge for Celtic as they ended a barren spell of six years without a trophy.

When I look at the club now and the unprecedented success they have had in the 21st century, it would be impossible to reconcile such a barren period with their fanbase.

Celtic were, quite literally, another step in my education. This was where I learned to speak English, drive a car and purchased my first house. Those were three things that would have been impossible in the Albania in which I grew up.

I was at the club at a really interesting and, looking back, somewhat fearful time for the great name of Celtic.

There are various stories about how close the club actually came to going out of business and believe me, you could sense the fear around the place at the time.

It was an unspoken fear, but it was there nonetheless and not just because of the club's standing in the world.

We are talking people's livelihoods and wages here. Mortgages to be paid, children to raise. I sometimes think that gets forgotten in the narrative of that period.

Fergus McCann it was who arrived with a bold plan and, more importantly, the finance to back it up with and there, my friends, lay the roots of the modern Celtic.

The stadium, under construction when I played there, is a breathtaking venue, particularly on a European night; and yet, for all that, I would still have missed 'The Jungle' – that special place where the roar of the lion could be heard.

So close to the pitch – so close to the players, that you could hear someone shouting your name as you hared down the touchline with the ball at your feet.

I have said it before and I will say it again, that was the heart and soul of Celtic Football Club to me.

There was the spot where the ordinary working man or woman could stand, support their team, but crucially, have a more intimate relationship with the players.

The camaraderie was outstanding. Honest. Wholehearted. Above all, genuine.

The club is almost unrecognisable from my time there as now it is a vast, wealthy beast, but at the conclusion of any day, it is the support that will always define Celtic to me.

I had my highs and lows in my time there and I am now on record as saying I was upset to leave.

However, I left in the knowledge that Rudi Vata had, as Liam Brady might have put it, 'done a job' for Celtic.

The support would have known that and, even now, when I go about the city, you will always have a supporter or two hailing me with a wave and a shout.

I do miss the jungle chant though of *RU-DI! RU-DI! RU-DI!*

***

The contrast between Glasgow and Limassol could not have been starker, of course. The heat, the temperature, the beach lifestyle – you rarely get that in the west of Scotland.

I started off thinking that Cyprus may have been a mistake on my part as it just didn't seem like a good fit for the culture of football, but I came to really enjoy my two years there.

Playing good football helps, of course, but on a personal level for me and Annfrances, it provided an opportunity.

She ran her own hairdressing business under her own steam for the first time and I could relate to the fact that it is an important thing to be the owner of oneself.

I saw a different side to the game with early morning and late evening training. The different conditioning that you had to do to your body to play out in that searing heat and the different tactics employed to run a game.

Under manager Momcilo 'Moka' Vukotic I started to become a bit more tactically aware.

I could also feel the pressure of being one of the foreign players on whose shoulders the supporters and your team-mates rested their hopes.

Of course, as an Albanian, I was always going to be an outsider at *any* club although there is, I feel, a similar approach to the Greek/Cypriot mentality and that of my own country so, perhaps in a way, I fitted in better in Limassol than I was ever going to do anywhere else.

Not winning a trophy was disappointing though as I had done so both at Dinamo Tirana and Celtic, but the overall experience of Cyprus was an enjoyable one – even with the odd earthquake thrown into the equation!

* * *

Germany was where I grew up both as a player and an individual. Out of all my time in the game, the period at Energie Cottbus was the most rewarding and not just because I was a part of the history-making squad who got promoted to the Bundesliga 1 for the first time.

No, Germany absolutely suited my views on life and football.

Discipline.

Hard work.

Complete mental awareness.

Independence.

Be a team player but be true to yourself as well.

Eduard Geyer was one of the most interesting people I ever met and certainly working with him was quite an experience.

Man-motivation over tactics.

Think about what you say – and then say it anyway!

We related to each other completely.

From the moment he made that point to me about Germany having an *actual* Franz Beckenbauer and for me to start thinking about what I could show him to prove my worth in his team, I grew into a different player.

I took to the German lifestyle so easily. It was a fast-paced country with a surging economy and the rewards for even a Bundesliga 2 player were exemplary.

That full season I had in the German top tier would definitely rank as my favourite time in the game.

The standard was so high.

Going into battle against clubs like Borussia Dortmund, Hamburg, Schalke and Bayern Munich is where you find out what kind of player you really are – what kind of individual.

There was no room to cower away in that league because you would soon be found out. For someone like me, who relishes a challenge, it brought out the best in me.

Energie Cottbus were, perhaps a bit like Celtic, born out of a tougher environment and that maybe contributed to their sense of having to fight to prove that you were worth your place at the top table.

We fought like lions for Eduard Geyer and, if we didn't?

Well, there was always the early morning run around the lake after a six-hour bus journey, in the dead of winter, listening to the wolves' howls under the moonlight!

It was a good time to be alive and play my football and, perhaps, this is where Rudi Vata peaked as a player.

To be named six times over the course of a season in the Bundesliga 1 starting XI by the respected sporting journal *Kicker* was testimony enough to me that I had done well for the club and the support.

* * *

The downside of Germany, of course, was the last few months of the season at Leichtatletik Rasensport Ahlen when I did not really enjoy my football and the club missed out on promotion.

I knew it was time for a change, but that change could not have been more considerable than our journey to east Asia after that short time back in Tirana.

My arrival into Japanese football was in that zone when the sport was having an increasing impact on the people of the country, and they were buying into it enthusiastically.

I loved their respect, honesty and the inner peace that all seemed to come easily to them as if was a part of their own DNA – perhaps it is.

The principles of the Yokohama supporters were quite unlike anything I had ever seen before and there was a reassurance that any performance out on the pitch would be treated courteously by the fans in the stadium.

I sometimes feel we could learn a lot from their approach to the game and life itself.

Working with Pierre Littbarski was, naturally, something that I was not going to turn down.

He immersed himself in the culture of the country and he was embraced by the support.

His qualities as a manager were self-evident in his teams.

He demanded that rigorous German discipline that I had seen in his own country but also outlined the rewards to those who would play to his tactics and work ethic.

As such, he was a class act.

Tokyo itself may have been the biggest cultural shock to my father and I have already talked about his wonderment at the billions of lights that lit up the city in a constant barrage of neon.

That has been one of the absolute joys of my football journey – the chance to share these experiences, these places with the very people who had given me a start in life: my parents.

My father was an intelligent man, but being of that older generation of Albanians, he would never have conceived that he would travel to places such as Japan and have the freedom to walk around a city like Tokyo.

I have never taken for granted what my parents did for me and Aleks and, in these moments, when I could take them to other parts of the world as well as taking other parts of the world to their door, were the rewards for a lifetime of love and a nod to my heritage. We never spoke about it directly, but I am sure, in my father's heart, he could see that I had made the right decision in Paris on that night in 1991.

There was precious little light in the Shkoder he knew and here now, in Tokyo, there was a sky full of it above our heads.

* * *

St Johnstone ended my playing days, of course, but in that brief time with the club, I believe I was shaping my decision to leave the game.

I had a handle on it and, as I say, it was a peaceful agreement with myself that my time was up.

I could now look back at a career that had taken me all the way from the city of my birth to various clubs around the world and shared so many different experiences.

Do I consider myself fortunate to have travelled and played in so many different environments?

Yes, of course.

The dream of the young Albanian boy was to play football.

The next dream was to play for my country.

But the ultimate dream – the dream that one dare not announce in the Albania of my youth – was to travel abroad and play the game.

I am a child of my time and that time saw the upheaval of a rigid, totalitarian system that stifled creativity, freedom and the right to ambition.

When I return to Albania now, I can see the progress.

The country that would not allow long locks and facial hair now has young men walking about with ponytails and beards.

The system that would not allow a second language now has a populace, notably under a certain age, who speak English fluently as well as other languages.

The next step for my country is to make the world feel that they are welcome in Albania.

A nation that for 45 years had a closed-border policy has opened that door and is looking for the world to come and embrace it.

We were taught as childen that Albania was the most beautiful country in the world and that we were lucky to live there.

In a sense, that was true.

Albanian coasts have always had the soft, sandy beaches, the blue water of the sea and a melting summer sun.

They have always had the beauty of the mountains that, although used for hidden terrors during the communist time, remained stoic and intact.

Here, we could look to build winter sports.

The cities are starting to thrive, and my native Shkoder is an interesting place to visit.

The only thing my country lacked was the infrastructure, but that is coming.

The Albania of say, five or ten years' time will be a different one than it is now, and it will be built on the backs of the young.

My boys Ruan and Rocco are frequent visitors to Shkoder. They listen as I point out the changes to them and I brought them both up to understand their heritage. I came from here and that part of my life that drove me on with the spirit to succeed against the odds is in their genetic make-up because of it.

Is there still corruption?

Of course there is, and I have been called out for complaining about the inward-looking nepotism of modern political life there, but hopefully, given time even that may change.

All I truly know is that the austerity and communism of the past has been replaced and the country in which Rudi Vata was born and raised – the country in which I dared to dream of ambition – is now a better place for others to dream, plan and enjoy.

CHAPTER 23

# RIDING OUT THE STORM

*Remember – even a storm will tire, and you must ride it out until that moment.*

*Then, the days will be normal.*

The words of my father from those moments as we walked across the beach on the coast of the Adriatic have stayed with me always, throughout my journey.

I have trusted in my instinct – trusted in God – and trusted in nature.

Nature teaches us that, to become a tree, you first must place the seeds down in the mother earth before they can grow upwards and out.

Two directions.

Upwards and then out.

The storms can pull you down but that is when the seed is fertilised and can make the journey back up.

Critically, if the roots of the tree are strong enough then they can withstand anything that life chooses to throw at it.

Upwards and then out.

Two directions.

In a sense, two lives in one lifetime.

And that is nature.

God?

God is all around us and I have been fortunate to recognise that presence on my journey.

When I look back to that time when I became a refugee in the camp in Nantes, I was surrounded by so many others.

I connected with quite a few of them and we had what we called a 'siege mentality'.

It was us against the world or, at least, the world we had come from, and we were making pacts with each other not to go back to that world.

I was determined on two fronts.

Not to go back and to move forward.

All I had was my skill out on a football pitch and all I wanted was a trial with a French club to start facilitating the next stage on my journey.

When that opportunity arose for me with Le Mans, I grabbed it.

In such circumstances, I may even have made a pact with the devil to set me free and get on that new path to freedom.

Before I left the camp, I was presented with new football boots by some of my fellow refugees.

I had my original boots, but they wanted to give me these new boots.

It was a fantastic gesture, but of course, I knew the boots had been purloined from somewhere.

Nobody in that camp was in a position to go out and pay money for football boots. They were stolen from somewhere, but in the spirit of camaraderie, I accepted them and decided that, when the Le Mans trial started, I would wear the boots gratefully.

And I did.

But then came that moment.

That moment when I went in on that tackle with Joel Bossis and my ankle cracked.

The ligaments were torn.

The ankle broken.

My new football boot split apart, and I watched as my ankle filled with blood.

As I lay on the ground, sick with agony at my immediate medical prognosis and the possibility that I might not be able to fulfil my destiny in professional football and gain my freedom, I looked up at the sky.

And I felt the presence of God.

The stolen boots were part of the pact with the devil.

I had worn boots that were not mine to have as I had not earned them and now I was being punished for that weakness.

I knew this as a certainty.

It was a sign.

I must follow a path.

Maintain my good habits and lose any bad ones.

God would be there with me, if I remained true to that path.

As another sign, I was delivered into the hands of other saviours.

They were named Bernard and Martine Lory and this couple lived in Mulsanne, Le Mans, France.

They were truly saviours for me.

Bernard was a football coach and he had seen my plight and offered to help me.

It was an amazing gesture.

I was taken into their home and nursed back to health.

Martine cooked for me, washed my clothes and became, in fact, just like a mother to me.

For three months I was under their roof and under their care and, in my journey, I want to acknowledge their impact on me.

They had a son, Jean, and he went on to become a football coach as well.

Whilst Martine would tend to this Albanian refugee who had come into their lives, Bernard would talk to me, encourage me, remind me that I was just on the start of something and I must stay strong.

I still keep in touch with them, and I still believe that God sent them to me at the time when I most needed someone to help me.

Another I would like to acknowledge from that time is, of course, my friend, Jean Rene Belliard.

He was another from that period of my life in France without whom I perhaps would never have progressed.

His wisdom, his financial acumen and let's not forget, his aptitude to make a telephone call to Celtic Park in Glasgow, were all things that quite literally changed my life.

The Lorys, Jean Rene – good people who just wanted to help without any reward for themselves.

Such people are God-given, I believe.

Then there were the football people from my earliest days in the game. People such as Selami Dani and Agim Medja who have not been mentioned so far in this narrative – but they were there in the beginning.

They recognised that this boy who had started out in the soil, barefooted, kicking a ball and working on his game, had talent and they nurtured that in my earliest days.

They taught me so much in the pre-Tirana days when I was aged 9–14.

Five years in a young boy's life when their influence and encouragement were immense as they taught me the ABC of football.

The XYZ, of course, as I have already stated, came from Aurel Verria, 'Coach Verria' who had me between 14 and 18 in Tirana at Loro Borici school.

Selami and Agim had me on the ground floor, but it was Coach Verria who took me to the next level.

He was my mentor in those times, building me up both physically and spiritually.

Mentality.

Character.

Personality.

I always return to those qualities in my life, and they started in Tirana under the tutelage of this remarkable man.

A man who dedicated himself to football and the development of those who he could see had a future in the game.

At that early age, I had been identified as a leader by Coach Verria and he was my mentor.

More than that, even – a father figure to me.

I have already used the word 'orphan' to describe this period in my life for that is what I was, in a sense.

Cut off from my family, determined to make my own way, but still in need of that guidance and authority that can only come from a parent.

In those four years of my youth, Aurel Verria became that 'parent' to me, and I thank him for it.

As I also do to Astrit Hafizi – Professor Astrit Hafizi.

Where would my journey have been without this man in my life?

He saw me at 18, gave me my debut and monitored my progress.

I asked him recently when I was back in Shkoder, what he had seen in me at that age that made him do these things and he replied by telling me that it was obvious to him that I was a 'leader'.

Someone he could trust out on the park to be the best version of myself.

He had seen qualities in me and determined that I could do a job for him. Of course, I was raw.

At that age, one is, but he took that rawness and helped me to mould it.

Our journey continued when he was with the national team.

As assistant to Bejkush Birce, he was there that night in Paris when I perhaps showed my ultimate role as a leader by leaving the Concorde Montparnasse Hotel, walking into a Gendarmerie and asking for my freedom.

He never questioned it, but as I have already highlighted, draped an arm around my father later and allowed him the gift of sobbing gently on his shoulder.

I repeat that he also made me his captain when he was in complete charge of the Albanian national side.

It was a further landmark in my journey and a further sign that he still trusted me to do that job.

Success to me is being accepted – respected.

In my travels, I have aimed for that acceptance and respect.

What was I to make of Scotland when I arrived at Celtic with my Ruud Krol long hair and out-of-date clothes??

This strange country with its driving on the wrong side of the road and the weather that could see one training in the searing heat one minute and then having relentless rain falling on to you out of the sky the next!

This was where I learned my English and learned what it was like to be part of an elite club – a player for Celtic Football Club.

I worked with great people there and will not forget them.

To single out one, in particular, is always a difficult choice but I want to thank my friend and my captain Paul McStay for penning the words at the start of my book.

He was approached and when asked to do so, he replied instantly, *yes!*

I am on record as highlighting what a great player he was and also a role model. Celtic were blessed to have him as the ultimate professional footballer.

In his time at the club, he saw the best of it and the worst of it, but never gave up and never flagged from being that special individual that you don't really see in the game much these days – a one-club man.

I repeat, he could have played *anywhere* but he remains a Celtic icon, a great name at the club and is revered as, quite simply, *The Maestro!*

Thank you, Paul.

In terms of this book, I must also thank Jane Camillin at Pitch Publishing who believed enough in my story to want to put it into print and also to Duncan Olner, who designed the distinctive sleeve of my book to combine my time as a footballer and reflect the times and the country that I came from.

Annfrances and I were introduced to Gerard McDade through a mutual friend, John Craig, who takes charge of the Celtic superstores. We were in one day and Annfrances mentioned that I was contemplating writing a book but would need someone to help when John replied, *I know a guy.*

That guy has turned out to be Gerard and, it was obvious to both Annfrances and me from his initial writings that he got both me and my story.

He came to Albania to see the places that he was writing about and take in a flavour of the country and the politics that I sprang from and has pursued my journey meticulously.

Through endless coffees, a few meals and a glass or two of wine, he has charted my story and I thank him for it.

And then there is family. First of all, my parents. It saddens me that my father, Pjeter, did not live long enough to see my story put into print as he passed away in the late summer of 2023, but my mother has been able to see my journey documented.

What can one say about one's parents?

They instilled qualities, life qualities in both myself and Aleks that allowed us to mature and develop.

Their lives have been happy ones, even those years spent under the yoke of the communist regime, and they never complained about their lot.

Aleks and I have learned so much from them.

Above all, they allowed us to be the people we wanted and needed to be.

My father would have known that there were absolutely no guarantees in pursuing a career in football, especially in the Albania that he knew.

In a sense, I would have gone against his wishes by doing so and he could have dictated to me on the subject, but crucially, he chose not to.

He identified my drive and my passion.

Both my parents did, and they allowed me to trust in my instinct and follow it through.

They equipped us for life and, as I will never forget, showed us a different path, even to the extent of risking the wrath of the communists by smuggling that Italian priest Uncle Ndreka into our house so that my brother and I could have access to another language.

They may well have known then of the paths we would follow.

Of course, their lives changed dramatically at the same time as Aleks' and mine when we sought our freedom.

When Aleks jumped on to that ship bound for Bari in Italy and then they received that letter from me telling them that I too was looking for my freedom, it must have been an incredibly bittersweet time for them.

Their boys were leaving and although I have always believed we had their blessing to do so, they were facing up to uncertainty.

It was all very well for me to say that I would send for them, but, given the background they had lived through with the closed borders of their country, it may have been something that they would not have believed.

I can understand that, but I did fulfil my promise to them and, thanks to God, I have been able to show them a world that they would not have thought possible.

It seems the least I could do to repay them for their guidance and faith.

And what of Aleks?

He too has made a life for himself.

From that time when he made the incredible 12-hour journey by train up to France we have both been free men.

He came to Scotland to live with me in December 1995 and looked after my house when Annfrances and I went to Cyprus for two years.

Like me, he is imbued with a work ethic that saw him take on a job as a mechanic in a garage in nearby Bellshill, working for a friend of mine named Ronny Campbell; move to Flintshire in Wales for a while to run a pub; and finally settle into a career with his own driving school in Glasgow.

Along the way, he has fathered two sons, Marco and Luka, and they remain close to my family and my sons.

Our journey has been, in so many ways, a shared one and our freedom is never taken for granted by those two boys who played together in the streets of Shkoder.

He is proud of what I have achieved in life, and I am equally as proud of him.

And then, there is my immediate family.

In Annfrances, I have had the perfect life partner.

I have always felt that we connected immediately on matters of family, especially.

Looking back to that night in December 1995 when we met, I remember how the boy from Albania, separated from his parents and his roots, found a kindred spirit in this girl from Wishaw who, with her deep Scots-Irish heritage, embraced the idea of family.

What a journey we have been on since then.

She was with me when my Celtic dream was coming to a sad end and then right there with me through Cyprus, Germany and Japan.

My success is our success as Annfrances immediately bought into my life almost as a nomad football player.

Wherever I could play, I would go, and she would come with me.

Our meeting was God-sent, and we have tried to stay true to the good fundamentals in life and our love of it.

A huge part of that life is taken up with our boys, Ruan and Rocco, and the joy we have had seeing them grow and develop into the young men they have become.

They are just starting the next chapters in their own journeys and Annfrances and I have faith in them to make the right choices.

The thread of family has run right through my life.

My parents.

My big brother, Aleks.

The father figure that was Coach Verria.

The Lorys in France who were my saviours as well as my adopted family.

The Murrays of Wishaw who took me as their son-in-law.

And, of course, Annfrances, Ruan and Rocco.

In life, one must be true to God, and one must be true to one's family.

There are good times and there are difficult times but one must navigate them.

At the start of this book, I gave you my beliefs.

It wasn't your fault if you were born into a country under dictatorship, but it was if you chose to accept it.

It wasn't your fault if you were born into poverty, but it was if you chose to do nothing about it.

Ultimately, freedom is choice.

As my father said to me:

*Remember – even a storm will tire, and you must ride it out until that moment.*

*Then, the days will be normal.*

And I listened.